1,001 Things You MUST Do Before You Get Married

THIS IS A CARLTON BOOK

Design, text and illustration copyright © Carlton Books Limited, 2001

This edition published by Carlton Books Limited 2001
20 Mortimer Street
London W1T 3JW

A CIP catalogue record for this book is available from the British Library.

ISBN 1 84222 403 4

Editorial Manager: Venetia Penfold
Art Director: Penny Stock
Project Editor: Zia Mattocks
Production: Garry Lewis
Illustrations: Mikki Rain

Printed and bound in Great Britain

Author credits

Thank you to Antoinette Azzurro, Gayle Chambers, Anne Crumpacker and her class in Dallas, Basia Gibson, Christina Hopkinson, Lizzie Kemp-Welch, Jamie Linville, Ben Moor, Eloise Napier, Nancy Shelton, Olivia Stewart-Liberty and any other friends I have forgotten who let me pick their brains!

1,001 Things You **MUST** Do Before You Get Married

clare de vries

CARLTON
BOOKS

1 Send a friend a
kissogram.
A1 Absolute Grams, 0800 3893857

2 Watch *Sex and the City*
on Channel 4 *religiously.*
It's the ultimate thirtysomething's guide to life.

Take a leaf out of
3 Charlie's Angels
and empower yourself.
Learn to kickbox.
All Stars Gym, (020) 8960 7724

4 *Throw a party for no good reason.*

5 Go riding down
Rotten Row.
Hyde Park Stables, (020) 7723 2813

6 Snog a pop star.

7 Be **sensual**

– don't just go for his dong *immediately*.

Tease him.

Kiss him on his other erogenous zones:
*nipples, ear lobes, neck, belly button,
armpits, insides of thighs …*

8 Photocopy your

boobs

on the office photocopier.

*Then fax them to your most important client
(after you've handed in
your notice, rather than before).*

9 Sleep with the boss.
Sexy? Yes. Sensible? No.

10 *Sleep under the stars.*

11 Make sure that at the beginning of your relationship you feel butterflies in your stomach, *bounce in your heart* and bubbles in your brain.
Marriage can be hard and sometimes the memory of your initial bond will be all you have to get you through.

12 Go for the super-kitsch approach to sex and imitate Hugh Hefner or Peter Stringfellow: *do it on satin sheets – black ones if possible.*

13 Smoke a joint.

(14) Get drunk on
tequila-and-champagne
slammers.

This is a particularly lethal combination
that induces an immediate
and massive high.

For other excellent cocktails
try Nam Long, (020) 7373 1926

(15) *Adopt a stray*
kitten or puppy,

so you can understand what it's like to
be responsible for the life of another.
It's good kiddie practice, too.

Battersea Dogs Home, (020) 7622 3626

(16) Live alone,

even if it's just for a few months.

Know that you can be independent.

17 *Learn to drive.*
Then pass your test.
BSM, 0845 7276276

18 Visit the luxury spa,
Chiva Som, in Thailand.
Treat yourself. You'll come home feeling like a million dollars.
They specialize in Thai and Swedish massages and also offer iridology, equilibropathy and energy healing.
Chiva Som, reserv@chivasom.co.th

19 Save some *money.*
Open a bank account
you can't touch for six months.

20 **Try the Hay Diet.**
Also known as Food Combining, this is the one where you avoid eating protein and carbohydrates at the same time.
So no meat and potatoes.
Either meat. *Or potatoes.*
But not both.

21 Live with *friends.*
Learn what it's like to have someone
else in your space, eating your food,
running up the phone bill and forgetting
to wash out the bath.

The upside is that there's
always someone to talk to,
and lots of spontaneous fun.

22 Leave lipstick
on a collar

– preferably with long-lasting gloss.

23 *Have sex wearing a*
femidom.

(And wonder how he keeps his erection
when confronted with what looks like a
dustbin liner sticking out of your fanny.)

24 Have a crush on
Marilyn Monroe.

*Copy her **make-up** and wear a **tight top**,
stilettos and a **billowing skirt** for a day.*

25 Swim in British
   coastal waters

– the beaches off Suffolk are lovely.
It's good for the circulation,

honest.

26   Have sex with
   someone with a very

large penis.

Just so you know what it's like …

27 Visit the Bliss Spa
   at 568 Broadway in New York.
   Bliss Spa, (00 1) 212 219 8970

28 Spend Saturday morning
wandering down

Bond Street

pretending you can afford

the clothes there.

*Gawp at the window displays of Chanel,
Donna Karan, Ralph Lauren and
Tiffany's, and see how the other half lives.*

29 # Get

therapy.

Get rid of those **niggling**
issues *that might rear their heads
and destroy a perfectly good
relationship. And get to
know yourself really well.*

30 *Try new positions:*
have sex with him sitting on a chair.
Climb on board!

31 Learn to
scuba
dive.
London Scuba Diving School, 07000 272822

32 *Travel alone.*
It's the ultimate in
independence
and self-sufficiency.

The downside: working out how to
cancel credit cards and inform the police
that your bag's been stolen when you don't
speak the language. The upside: you
can do what you want when you want.

33 Try CAT

(coital alignment technique):

it improves the chance of simultaneous orgasms.

His pelvis should be on top of yours and his full weight on you (not on his elbows). You both rock and roll at the same time so that he inserts on your upward movement and comes out, his shaft pressing against your *mons veneris*, on the downward movement.

34 *Have your heart broken*

so you know what rejection's like.

Then resolve to end affairs kindly, face to face and with respect.

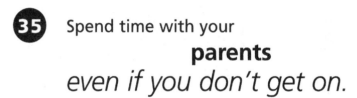

35 Spend time with your
parents
even if you don't get on.
They're not around for ever and even
if your personalities clash, you still
love each other deep down.
Try and show it.

36 Know which
contraception
suits you
– and don't rely on a man to take it.
Be responsible for your own pregnancy
scares. ALWAYS go on a date armed
with a condom – just in case.

37 # *Dye your hair*
blonde – or brown if you're already blonde.
And find out if blondes
really do have more fun.

38 # Join a gym.

Recent research shows that three sessions of
30-minute cardiovascular exercise per
week combats stress and is as effective
for lifting depression as drug therapy.

39 ## Throw away *all* diet books.

40 # *Know his limits.*

Don't take him shopping on
Oxford Street for **six hours** on
a Saturday if **two hours** are as
much as he can take.

41 Try new positions: do it doggy style
and howl like a wolf.

42 ## Eat at Maxim's in Paris
*for the ultimate in art deco,
jet-set dining elegance.*
Maxim's, (00 33) 1 42 65 27 94

43 Wander around
Portobello market
on a Saturday morning.
(And not just because of the film Notting Hill.)
Although bargains are now harder to
find, there still remains excellent silver,
lace and unusual antique stalls.

44 Eat at one of England's best restaurants.
Le Manoir Aux Quatre Saisons
in Oxfordshire.
Le Manoir Aux Quatre Saisons, (01844) 278881

45 *Take the* Eurostar
to Paris
with girlfriends for the weekend.

Stay at the Hotel Costes
if you're splashing out.
Otherwise, just go there for a cocktail.
Eurostar, 0870 5186186;
Hotel Costes, (00 33) 1 42 44 50 00

46 Ask him whether he'd consider
taking the male pill.
(Not so as to make him take it but to hear
his answer: 'Yes' indicates an open, sensitive,
considerate soul and 'No' shows a more
macho, selfish streak.)

47 Complain in a restaurant.
And then leave.
*You don't want to eat whatever you
sent back – nine times out of ten
something nasty will have been done to it.*

48 Contemplate how *short*
life is, and visit
Highgate Cemetery.
Highgate Cemetery, (020) 8340 1834

49 *Have sex using a cock ring,*
available from any good sex shop.
*(It keeps the blood pressure in the
penis high, thereby prolonging the erection.)*

50 Cut your hair very short.
Toni & Guy, (020) 7637 2233

51 Dance on tables.

52 Look out for
King Kong
at the top of the Empire State Building.
**Empire State Building, (00 1) 212 736 7100,
extension 355 for group bookings**

53 # Get
sacked.

54 Learn to **ski**
if you can afford it

and experience the ultimate thrill and
exhilaration of inhaling squeaky-clean air
while sliding helplessly out of
control down a steep mountain on
two pieces of wood.
Ski World Tour, (020) 7602 4826

See the work of the
great British playwrights.
Go to the theatre and watch:

55 a *David Hare play*

56 a *Tom Stoppard play*

57 a *Harold Pinter play*

58 Do a bungee jump.

*Throwing yourself off a high platform
feels like one of the most unnatural
things in the world. But the sense
of achievement afterwards is magnificent.*

**www.adventurehandbook.com for info on
UK bungee jumping; UK Bungee Club at
Alexandra Palace, (020) 7731 5958**

59 Have the *best* coffee *ever*
at the Tazza d'Oro near
the Pantheon in Rome.

Tazza d'Oro, (00 39) 6 678 9792

Watch the *best* films ever:

60 *The Matrix* starring Keanu Reeves

61 *Terminator 1*
  starring Arnold Schwarzenegger

62 Then *Terminator 2,*
  straight after the first one

63 *Withnail & I* starring Richard E Grant
  – perfect for a Sunday afternoon

64 *Butch Cassidy and the
  Sundance Kid* – and swoon over
  Paul Newman and Robert Redford

65 *Cinema Paradiso*
  starring Philippe Noiret

66 *It's a Wonderful Life*
  starring James Stewart
– ideal when you're feeling grumpy and depressed

67 *Breakfast at Tiffany's*
  starring Audrey Hepburn

68 *The Godfather* starring Marlon Brando
  – and then talk like a gangster's moll
  for at least two hours afterwards

69 *Pretty Woman*
  starring Julia Roberts and Richard Gere

70 Get your hands *dirty*.
Change a tyre.

71 Wear a wig.
Reinvent yourself like Madonna
or Linda Evangelista
and be someone else for a night.

72 ***Give up artificial substances***
for a day: no painkillers,
no foodstuffs with *colourings,*
preservatives or flavours.

73 Choose from nine
delicious *foie gras* dishes at
Club Gascon in Smithfield Market.
Club Gascon, (020) 7796 0600

74 Vary your sex times: sometimes make it a
quickie, sometimes a
sexathon.

75 Call in sick
and spend the day being a
lady who lunches.

76 # Buy Chanel's
Extrait de Rouge – Extase
blood-red lipstick.

77 *Eat ice cream at the
Trevi Fountain in*
Rome.
The baroque architecture is
incredible and Italian ice cream is
a whole lot better than Wall's.

78 Ride on the back of a boy's scooter.

(Go to Rome to find the boy ...)

79 Now and then laugh at your man's jokes even when they're not that funny

or you've heard them before.
He may need an ego boost. Wouldn't you
like him to do the same for you?

80 *Jump the traffic*

by driving behind a wailing ambulance.

81 Have sex with his penis between your breasts.

Decency prevents me from using the street term for this.

82 Order all the chef's specialities at Le Grand Vefour in Palais Royale, Paris.

Then tip the bus boy 200FF to light the candles in
the garden for a magically romantic walk after dinner.

Le Grand Vefour, (00 33) 1 42 96 56 27

(83) *Get aggressive at go-karting.*

F1 City, (020) 7476 5678

(84) Change a plug.

And don't blow up the house while you're doing it.

(85) Fake an orgasm. And then say, *'Only kidding!'*

(86) *Get your nails manicured.*

For a quick fix, visit Nails Inc., e-mail info@nailsinc.com or telephone head office, (020) 7382 9542 for details of your nearest nail bar. Alternatively, visit Iris Chapple, the doyenne of fabulous nails, (020) 7486 6001

87 Go to New York for
at least a week. Then

shop, shop, shop.

Hot spots include Bloomingdales,
Henry Bendel and Barneys New York.

**Bloomingdales, (00 1) 212 355 5900;
Henry Bendel, (00 1) 212 247 1100;
Barneys New York, (00 1) 212 339 7300**

88 Drive up the
Californian
coast road (Highway 1)
in a classic convertible.

(89) **Skip the beach holiday**
and go for the desert –
the Atacama desert in Chile is pretty impressive.

(90) Shop in the souk in Marrakech
for carpets, hubble-bubble
pipes and richly-woven silks.
*The colours, smells and noise
are intense and fascinating.*
The Best of Morocco, (01380) 828533

(91) *Play an instrument.*

(92) Call someone you've
fallen out with.
*Life's too short to hold a grudge.
Be a big person, not a petty one.*

93

Sing at a karaoke bar.

Elvis always goes down well.

94

Do the Anapurna Trek
in Nepal

and reward yourself with one of those yak wool hats with the flaps.
It's a great way to meet fit, single guys, too.

95 **Try not to sleep with him
on the first few dates.**

That way you might have the time to work out that he just ain't worth it.

96 Visit Graceland in Memphis,
Tennessee, and pay homage to

Elvis.

Graceland, (00 1) 901 332 3322

97 *Improve your* sex life:
while he's inside you put your legs behind his ears *for deeper penetration, and pulse around his penis.*

98 Buy a **pair of gloves** from
Hèrmes.
Hèrmes, (020) 7499 8856

99 *Have a perfume specially created for* you by Frederic Malle *in Paris.*
Editions de Parfum Frederic Malle, (00 33) 1 42 22 77 22

100 Always be positive *before being negative.*

(101) Ride around
the Pyramids
in Egypt
on a camel.
Egyptian Tourist Board, 0900 1600299

102 Do a *Boys Don't Cry* thing and dress like a man for a day.

Do the walk, do the talk, do it all.
See what it's like to be a man.
(It's not always easy being the first
to call or ask for a date.)

103 Do *The Rules* on a boyfriend *and see if they work.*

(*The Rules* is by Ellie Fein and Sherrie Schneider.)

104 *Say 'yes'* to all invitations.
You never know what's out there:
new friends, new job offers
– you may even find love.

105 ***Try to get out of that ticket*** *by flirting with a traffic warden.*

(106) Breakfast on
papaya and pineapple
at the Oriental Hotel in Bangkok.
Oriental Hotel, (00 66) 2 236 0400

(107) *Make a list of*
everyone you've slept with.
Be proud of it. *(Then hide it.)*

(108) *Keep account of your*
bank and credit card statements.

(109) ***Learn how to read finance documents and legal reports.***

(110) Stand up a guy
who's treated you badly.

111 # Swallow.
(You know what I'm referring to.)

It doesn't have to be every time
if you don't like it, just now and
then so he doesn't feel rejected.

112   *Try Spa NK's*
La Stone Therapy

– a delicious full-body massage
using hot and cold stones.
Spa NK, (020) 7727 8002

113   Get a makeover from one of the
cosmetics assistants in Selfridges.
It's free!
Selfridges, (020) 7629 1234

114 Know **Harvey Nichols** inside out.

(The basement is for men – so ignore it.)
Ground floor – make-up and accessories.
First floor – heavy-duty designer clothes.
Second floor – Nicole Farhi, Joseph and other
more affordable designers.
Third floor – swimwear and casual stuff.
Fourth floor – homeware.
Fifth floor – food hall, fantastic restaurant
and cocktail bar
Harvey Nichols, (020) 7235 5000

115 Be unconventional:
buy your man flowers.
Interflora, 0500 871187

116 *Look after* a friend's
kids for the day.
You'll soon know whether you want
some yourself or not. Take the friend's mobile
number before they leave in case it turns out
that you're not Mary Poppins.
You might require back up.

117 *Ask a guy out*
before he asks you.

118 **Give up smoking**
– or drinking if you don't smoke.
Just for a while, just to see
if you can do it.

(Read Allen Carr's *Easy Way to Stop Smoking*.
If you're a really heavy drinker
try Alcoholics Anonymous.)
Alcoholics Anonymous, (01245) 256147

119 *Be a model for a day*
and have good portrait photos
taken of yourself. Phone a local
photographer for advice.

120 Go for
all-out pampering
and spend a day with friends at
The Sanctuary in Covent Garden.
The Sanctuary, (020) 7420 5151

121 Walk out of your job.
Tell your boss to
go stick it.
Throw your hands in the air, yell
'That's it!' and leave.

122 **Have fun and role-play in bed:** doctors and nurses; teachers and pupils; reluctant virgin and so on.

123 *Eat sushi.*

If you're feeling flash, eat it
with the glitterati at Nobu.

If you're not, learn how to make it yourself
from *The Sushi Cookbook* by Katsuji Yamamoto.
Nobu, (020) 7447 4747

124 Buy artwork
for your walls.

Ditch your Athena posters
and hit the galleries.

**(For more ideas, see
Living With Art by Karen Wheeler.)**

125 Go through an
organic phase

– and spend a fortune on your groceries.
Organic food is healthier for you as no
pesticides or unnatural additives or
processes are used. Most supermarkets
now have organic sections.

126 *Learn a poem off by heart.*

'If' by Rudyard Kipling
is good if you're in need of bolstering.

'*How do I love thee?
Let me count the ways*'
by Elizabeth Barrett Browning
is always a winner with couples.

127 Get as much
education as you can.

128 Know and *understand*
one Shakespeare play really well.

129 Try the Zone Diet.

*This is the one where you eat exactly
balanced proportions of carbohydrate,
protein and fat, according to your body weight.
The general thinking is that we eat much too
much carbohydrate in the West, and
the Zone Diet ups our amount of protein.*

Hit the dance floor

when you hear any of
these *seminal dance tracks:*

130 *'Things Can Only Get Better'*
by D-Ream

131 *'Ride on Time'* **by Black Box**

132 *'Turn Around'* **by Phats & Small**

133 *'Firestarter'* **by Prodigy**

134 *'The Theme from S Express'*
by S Express

135 *'White Lines'*
by Grand Master Flash and Melle Mel

136 *'You Don't Know Me'*
by Duane Harden

137 *'Renegade Master'* **by Wildchild**

138 *'Born Slippy'* **by Underworld**

139 *'Dancing Queen'* **by Abba**

140 *Relax*

by bathing in water with two handfuls of coarse sea salt added to it. It soothes the skin, draws out toxins and eases tense muscles.

141 Watch the summer opera from the big screen in Covent Garden plaza.

Royal Opera House, (020) 7240 1200 or www.royaloperahouse.org

142 Have your *teeth straightened or whitened* if they need it.

Lund Osler Dental Practice, (020) 7838 8969

143 Listen to *Beethoven's Emperor Concerto.*

144 # Attend the Palio
in Siena, Italy,

the annual horse race where 17
contestants gallop three laps
of the Piazza del Campo.

***There are very few rules in this race, which
is so competitive that kidnapping of
jockeys is not unknown.***

145 **Take note of your man's driving style.**

Do you like it?
Is it terrifying?

*Can you imagine him safely trolleying you
and the kids to the local swimming pool on Saturday
mornings? If you don't like the way he drives,
either come to terms with it, or ask
him (gently) to change his style.*

146 *Dress in a* colour
you've never worn before.

147 Sleep with a **French** or **Italian guy,**
and get over *that.*

148 *Have a one-night stand*
and refuse to give him your number.

149 Experience the
London Eye
with a group of friends.
**London Eye, 0870 4003005 for group bookings
or 0870 5000600 for individual tickets**

150 Take a
young man's
virginity.
But don't expect the session to last long.

151 Don't let the one you
really fancy get away.
When you're married you
don't want to think,
'Ooh, I wish I'd nailed so-and-so ...'

152   ## Live abroad for a while.
It's lonely at first but it's character building.

153   ## Play **Vivaldi's** *Gloria*
at full blast on a Sunday morning.

154   # *Go on a*
24-hour fast.
Drink three pints of fluid while you do it
so as not to get dehydrated.
You'll feel lean and clean afterwards.

155   ## See *Swan Lake* live.

156   Enhance your health and
prolong your life by practising
ayurveda,
India's ancient holistic lifestyle.
**For ayurvedic beauty treatments contact
Bharti Vyas, (020) 7935 5312 or
www.bharti-vyas.com; for further
information call the Ayurvedic Company
of Great Britain, (020) 7224 6070**

157 *Watch a* lion
hunt gazelles
on the Serengeti.

158 Go punting
with friends
on the Cherwell river
in Oxford and
picnic on
champagne
and strawberries
and cream.

Read some nutty
South American literature:
*anything by Isabel Allende
or Gabriel García Márquez, for example.*

 Explore **Tantric sex**
with your loved one for **prolonged**
orgasms, **increased** energy levels and
connection to the **Tao** (in other
words, being at one with the world).

Check out the website: tantric.com

 Do **Kegels exercises.**
(they tighten the vaginal muscles)

It's the same action as when you
stop peeing. Pull up inside yourself
and hold it for a count of five. Do this
ten times twice a day to begin with and,
as you get stronger, work up to 20 reps
and alternate between holding it for
between two and ten seconds.

*(The good thing is you can do your exercises on
the bus into work and no one will ever know.)*

162 *Go to the*
Glastonbury Festival.

And take your wellies in case it turns into a mud bath.

Glastonbury Festival, (0115) 9129129

163 Buy yourself a proper
stereo with
good speakers.

*(Denon, Sony and Aiwa are good
affordable brands. Bang & Olufsen
is excellent but expensive.)*

164 Play Rachmaninoff's
Concerto no.3
at top blast when feeling low.

165 *Accept
yourself.*

166 Dress like a slut

– micro miniskirts, fishnets, tight cropped tops, stilettos.

167 *Drink*

a hot chocolate

at Les Deux Magots on St Germain des Prés in Paris while reading a book in French.

Les Deux Magots, (00 33) 1 45 48 55 25

168 Buy yourself *red roses.*

169 *Read the newspapers*

– and not just *The Sunday Times.*

170 *Masturbate.*

171 Masturbate him.
(Learn more than one method.)

172 Be passionate about something.
Anything.
And don't go halfway.
Go all the way with it.

173 Ask someone famous for their autograph.

174 Watch a horror film by yourself
on a cold winter's night.
(The Exorcist, The Omen or The Shining will do the trick.)

175 Declaim at Speaker's Corner in
Hyde Park.

⓱⓶ Get on TV
– even if it's just as part
of a studio audience.

⓱⓷ Eat at the Ivy restaurant
in Covent Garden,
regular stomping ground of the luvvies.
Ivy, (020) 7836 4751

⓱⓸ *Try Thai food*
– it's more interesting than Chinese.

⓱⓹ Treat yourself
to a pashmina.

They're great (and very soft) wraps for any
occasion, smart or casual. Better still, they
can be worn all year round and come in every
colour under the sun. They're affordable
now, too. Get yours from Marks and Spencer ...

180 Spend a Sunday
doing nothing
but watching
Simpsons or *Friends* videos.

181 *See your favourite*
comedian live.

182 Watch the sunset
from the comfort of a felucca gently
drifting down the Nile.

183 Book yourself into
St Martin's Lane Hotel
in London and play with the
multicoloured lighting system.
St Martin's Lane Hotel, (020) 7300 5500

184 Take the funicular up Castle Hill in
Budapest
and enjoy panoramic views of
the city and river Danube.

185 See an
eclipse.

186 *Learn to meditate.*

*Find a quiet warm room, sit comfortably,
breathe deeply and let your thoughts flow and
pass. Concentrate on your breathing. Five minutes
of meditation every day will help you to become
more focused and grounded.*

187 Give him a rim
– circle the world,
perhaps, is a more delicate way of putting it ...

188 Try yoga.

It's good for the mind, body and spirit

because it calms, stretches, detoxes, relaxes, tones and centres. It's also great for the posture. There are many different versions: *Ayenga*, *Vini* and *Hatha* to name but a few. Madonna is a big fan of the more dynamic version, Astanga.

The Life Centre, (020) 7221 4602; Triyoga, (020) 7483 3344; for more information and classes in your area contact The British Wheel of Yoga, (01529) 306851

189 Do some community work: *shop for* pensioners.

190 ## Wear Elvis knickers.

Or Bart Simpson knickers.

Just be sure you have
some *very silly knickers.*

191 ## Cook something
truly disgusting

and see how he responds.
If he loves you he'll find it charming.

192 *Suck someone off at work.*

193 When you've found someone to love,

make sure he's not gay.

Test him by suggesting an evening in a gay night club. If he's really keen, you should probably think twice ...

194 Work out how compatible you are: **is he extrovert or introvert** *and what about you?*

If he's extrovert, are you invigorated or exhausted by his energy? And vice versa.

195 Have good sex *with the one you think is Mr Right.*

If it's not good before the wedding, it won't be afterwards either.

Don't take any risks.

Remember what happened to Charlotte in *Sex and the City*.

196 *Find out if he's a dog or a cat person. If you're the opposite, think again.*
Bad scene.

197 *There are two types of people in this world.* Those who like Gregorian chants and
those who don't.
Find out which he is and make sure you're both on the same side of
that one.

198 # Share a bathroom
with a man before marrying him.
Or fit your bathroom with two basins.
Keep an eye on those bad habits: does he rinse the basin after shaving, put the loo seat down and flush every time? If not, can you train him up? Or, alternatively, put up with his slobbishness?

Improve your mind
with these all-time classics:

199 *Anna Karenina* by Tolstoy

200 *Tess of the D'Urbevilles*
by Thomas Hardy

201 *Madame Bovary* by Gustave Flaubert

202 *Jane Eyre* by Charlotte Brontë
– then, reader, marry him

203 *Dangerous Liaisons*
by Choderlos de Laclos

204 *Middlemarch* by George Eliot

205 *Pride and Prejudice* by Jane Austen

206 *Great Expectations*
by Charles Dickens

207 *Portrait of a Lady* by Henry James
– just don't make the same mistake
she did with regard to marriage

208 *Vanity Fair* by William Makepeace
Thackeray – not the magazine

209 Get a subscription to

Vanity Fair,

*the magazine, not the book
by William Makepeace Thackeray.*

It'll give you dinner party conversation topics for weeks to come.

210 Watch the movie
The Way We Were

with Robert Redford and Barbra Streisand. If he walks out, makes fun of Barbra's nose, rolls his eyes a lot or says 'C'mon man, you can do better!',

question his sensitivity.

211 Establish early on
who is *in* control
of the *remote* control.

A high percentage of divorces are caused by disagreement over what to watch on telly on any given night of the week.

212 Earn your own

money.

It will give you independence
and confidence.

213 Live on your own terms.
Do what *you* want to do.
You can compromise later.

214 Take a **road trip** together.
Or drive for eight hours.
Make sure you are temperature-
and radio-compatible.

215 Keep an eye on how he treats

his mother.

His attitude to women will be a
make-or-break factor in your marriage.

216 Keep an eye on how his mother *treats him* and his relationship with his mother in general. This will pretty much indicate whether he trusts women or not.

217 Have sex on your desk.

218 Let it all hang out. Play your music loudly.

219 *Learn to forgive and forget.*

220 Buy at least one
really great dress
(or perhaps four or five)
that makes you feel irresistible.

221 *Eat at The Connaught*
and enjoy the atmosphere of
old world, formal elegance.
The Connaught, (020) 7491 0668

222 Go on at least one
dirty weekend
to a dodgy British seaside town.

Hastings will do.

(Always take air freshener.
There are some bathroom activities that
are just too intimate and un-fragrant
for a new man to experience.)

223 Enjoy the particular challenges of your life: in other words, *'Face the music* **and dance.'**

224 Shag your cousin.

225 *Be here, now.*
Live in the moment. It may sound like Buddhist baloney, but it can have a surprisingly positive effect on your life.

226 Wake up in a strange bed, have no idea **where** you are or **who** or **what** is lying next to you.

227 **Have sex in broad daylight** on a beach.

228 *Write a book.*

If it gets published, that's great,
but the point is to write it and finish it.

229 Tie someone to your bed

for at least 24 hours.

230 *Binge on junk food.*

(231) Check out how your man is with your friends.

Does he make an effort with them or is he rude and dismissive? Worse, does he flirt with them? He doesn't have to like everyone – no one ever does – *but he does have to make an effort for your sake. If he doesn't, think again.*

(232) Have your portrait painted.
National Portraiture Association, (020) 7602 0892

(233) Go through all your cupboards, gather together a pile of old clothes you never wear and give them to *Oxfam.*

(234) Take a plane ride over the Grand Canyon.

235 Have your *hair cut* by Charles Worthington, snipper to the stars.

Charles Worthington, (020) 7631 1370

236 Go to the dogs.

Wimbledon Greyhound Track, (020) 8946 8000

237 *Sell something:*

your car, old clothes, cosmetics door-to-door …

238 *Gamble on the Grand National.*

Contact William Hill Helpline
for your nearest bookie, 0870 5181715

239 Go three in a bed.

240 Learn the meaning of
three obscure words
*(for instance sigil, thereman
and steatopygous),*
drop them into a dinner party
conversation and then watch everyone pretend
they know what you're talking about.

241 Wave goodbye to a dumpster with
the following words:
*'You haepogonadic
oleaginous moron.
You're history.
I'd rather be with
a barnyard animal.'*

242 Buy yourself a cashmere top:
– either a cardigan or jumper will do.
Good brands are Ballantyne and Brora.
Marks and Spencer also does a
good value line in cashmere.

243 Pick up a *gorgeous stranger*
in a bar and take him home.

(244) *Sleep starfish*
in the middle of the bed.
And enjoy it.
You won't be able to do it forever (hopefully).

(245) Let him go
to any sports
events he wants.
And use the time to see your friends.

(246) *Join the*
mile-high club.
(This means have sex in an aeroplane at
30,000 feet. You'll have to do it in the rather
cramped loo so as not to get arrested.)

(247) Gorge on chocolates while watching
Gone with the Wind.

248 Date **two** or more people **at the** same time.

249 *Swim with dolphins.*
Contact Bahamas Tourist Information,
(01483) 448900

250 Let him shave your pubes into a heart.
Or a thin landing strip.
Or a porn star postage stamp.
Or any other shape you can think of.

251 *Cook Christmas lunch for your Mum.*

252 Go on a yoga holiday with a girlfriend.
Triyoga, (020) 7483 3344; www.ulpotha.com;
Holistic Holidays, www.hoho.co.uk or
(020) 8241 3880; Free Spirit Travel, (01273) 564230

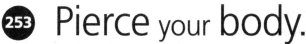

253 # Pierce your body.
Most people go for the belly button.
But if you're feeling brave
you could try a nipple.

254
Book into a hotel
just for sex.

255 ## Make sure you know
all his past BEFORE
you marry him. Try reading
Rebecca by Daphne du Maurier
if you need convincing further.

256 # Start a pension plan.
*Why should your husband
take on all the responsibility of
providing for the future?*
Independent Financial Advisers, (020) 7288 6400

257 Attend enough
weddings to know
what you want for your own
– *but don't daydream about it endlessly.*

258 *Play footsie*
at a dinner party
with the stranger opposite you.

259 **Spend all day in bed.**

260 Get a tattoo.

261 *Read a Mills and Boon
or Barbara Cartland novel.*

262 Have a competition with a friend to
snog the most boys at a party.

263 Go with lots of girlfriends
on a clubathon/shagathon
to Ibiza.
**Club Med, 0700 2582633 or www.clubmed.com;
to find the best sounds try
www.ministryofsound.com**

264 Sleep with someone of the
same sex.
That way, if it all falls apart and you
end up hating men, you'll know whether
or not you have an alternative
to look forward to.

265 *Wear nothing but a mac* to the supermarket.

266 *Cut up an ex's ties.*

267 Buy some *Playboy* cocktail glasses.
www.playboy.com

268 Go skateboarding with under-twentysomethings.

Be hip and au fait
with the cult films:

269 *Pulp Fiction* **starring John Travolta, Uma Thurman and Samuel L Jackson**

270 *Shampoo* **starring Warren Beatty and Julie Christie**

271 *Reservoir Dogs* **starring Harvey Keitel**

272 *Blade Runner* – the *Director's Cut* **starring Harrison Ford and Rutger Hauer**

273 *The Rocky Horror Picture Show* **starring Richard O'Brien**

274 *Apocalypse Now* **starring Marlon Brando and Martin Sheen**

275 *Taxi Driver* **starring Robert De Niro and a very young Jodie Foster**

276 *The Seven Samurai* **starring Toshiro Mifune**

277 *Thunderball* **starring Sean Connery**

278 *Easy Rider* **starring Dennis Hopper and Peter Fonda**

279 *Go through an incense stick/Indian wall hanging/yingy-yangy phase.*

280 # Be dominating.

Have your dirty way with him and don't take 'no' for an answer. Stay on top (facing him, facing away, lying full length on him) the entire time.

Pin him down ...

281 Say,

'I don't think so Sweet Meat,'

to some presumptuous boy.

282 Pretend you're # Madonna

and stay at Inverlochy Castle in Scotland for a night.

Inverlochy Castle, (01397) 702177

283   Buy some outrageously
                  sexy underwear
from Agent Provocateur.
Agent Provocateur, (020) 7235 0229

284 Open the
door to
him in
*pink stiletto
pompom
mules
and a
baby-doll
cream
lacy nightie.*

285 Say,
'Stuff a sock in it, upchuck,'
to a waiter with attitude.

286 *Pay for a male escort.*

287 Are you secretly hoping to be provided for by a man in the future?
Give this secret wish up! It's damaging to your independence.

288 Have an affair
with your yoga instructor/personal trainer.

289   *Have an* *orgasm* *on a train*.

290   **Sleep on the beach.**

291   Flash your tits at a policeman.

292   Go hot-air ballooning.
Acorne Sports, (01494) 880000

293   *Have sex in a doorway.*

294 # Fall in love
with someone who
can't speak a word
of English.

295 Buy a set of screwdrivers and
a cordless power drill and
put up your first set of
shelves or pictures.
*You'll soon discover you're
much better at DIY than him.*

296 Learn to *apologize.*

297 Buy a beautiful piece
of **furniture**
you completely love:
*an antique bed, walnut wardrobe or
modern glass table, for instance.*

298 Learn to confront *a lover or friend* without losing the lover or friendship.

299 *Have phone sex.*

300 Learn when to *work* at it and when to *walk* away.

301 Chuck out the 'Rescue Me' fantasy once and for all. You do not need a man to have a great life.

302 *Have internet sex.*

303 *Stop blaming your childhood.*

304 # Kick those addictions.

Smokers Quitline (020) 7487 3000; Alcoholics Anonymous, (01904) 644026

305 Think carefully about why you want to get married.

Ask yourself three questions:

1 Would you like your children to be like him?

2 Do you respect/like his attitudes/approach to life?

3 Do you just want to sleep with him?

306 Find out what the **Labour, Conservative** and **Liberal Democrat** parties *really stand for.*

307 Question your received set of values.

Not so as to reject them necessarily, but so as to be sure of what you really feel is right. It's so easy to believe the first thing you may hear, but it may not actually work for you.

308 Open an account at a really **good** florists and make sure he has the **number**. That way he need never turn up on your **doorstep** with *cheap garage flowers and a lame excuse.*

309 # Buy good jewellery.

He may be your knight in shining armour but his taste could just amount to 'poppet beads'.
(Buy affordable silver in India.)

310 ## Put money aside *now* for *plastic surgery.*

Men 'mature' with age while women 'fall apart'. (It may be an objectionable popular myth but it's out there and are you going to fight it alone?) He's not going to want to pay for your renovation or preservation.

311 ## Dump a friend (or anyone)

who makes you feel bad about yourself – who takes without giving or who points out your faults.

312 # Go
parachuting.
Acorne, (01494) 880000

313 Spend two weeks
completely
naked
on a Caribbean beach.

314 Learn to point out what irritates
you about your man gently.

Criticizing him **harshly** will hurt his
feelings, harm his **confidence** and
eventually **impinge** on your sex life.

315 Visit the *Taj Mahal*
at sunrise and full moon to
understand *the meaning of true love.*
It was built as a mausoleum
to the wife of Shah Jehan
who died in childbirth.

316 Buy lovely **linen** for your bed.
Cologne & Cotton, (020) 7486 0595

317 *Gorge on cakes*
filled with cream, jam and chocolate.

318 Go on a car
mechanic's
course.

It's incredibly liberating no longer
being ripped off by sexist mechanics.

The Floodlight *guide come out three times a year:*
April for the summer courses, July for the
part-time courses starting in September,
and October for the full-time courses.

Available from all good book shops
or from www.floodlight.co.uk

319 Hide **all self-help**
books *before inviting a date*
back to your home.

320 Become a **Sanyasin**
at the ashram in **Poona, India,**
and experience plenty of free
loving, thereby exhausting any urges
to be unfaithful when married.

321 Keep plants and
learn the joys of
responsibility
– or at least the joy of not being spoken back to.

322 Go out with *weirdos.*
Then you'll appreciate someone
nice when you meet him.

323 **Get tested for VD.**
(That's what you get for
going out with weirdos.)

**Phone your doctor's surgery or The Jefferiss Wing,
St Mary's Hospital, Paddington, (020) 7886 1697
for the number of a local STD clinic**

324 *Send Valentine cards*
to everyone you fancy.

325 When you've found him, set lots of
prenuptial
agreements
– not necessarily finance related – in order
to avoid disagreements later. Issues
to agree on include holidays, where to live,
who'll look after the kids and so on. Agree
verbally, and write them down if you have
to, so as to remind yourselves later.

326 *Sing loudly*
in the bath or shower.

327 Dance around naked
in your sitting room
before going out for
the evening.

328 Spend a Sunday morning
with *girlfriends* at the
Porchester Spa's wonderful
art deco *Russian steam* rooms
and *Turkish baths* in London.
Porchester Spa, (020) 7792 2919

329 # Don't believe
people who say,

'Size is unimportant, it's all technique'.

*Experience a few big ones so you can
tell them they're either stupid or lying.*

330 *Go to Rio
for the Carnival.*

331 Send a *romantic email*
to someone from
a colleague's computer
and watch the sparks fly.

332 Dress up in a wig
and funky clothes and

pretend you're someone else at a friend's party.
Introduce yourself to your friends and see
if they like you better this time around.
Ask them casually what they think of the 'real' you.

333 *After a boozy night, sweat out*
your toxins in a sauna.

If it was a really heavy night, don't stay
in there longer than ten minutes
or you might faint.

334 *Have sex on the*
number 6 bus
as it goes around *Piccadilly Circus.*
(Don't do this during rush hour,
however, or you may get arrested.)

335 *Surf* off Cornwall.

(Take your wetsuit. It's more than cold.)

Cornish Tourist Board, (01872) 322900

336 Hang out *with* musicians.

337 *Stop the car*
on the way back from a
weekend in the country ...

find a corn field
with a tractor/combine harvester
in it, and ...

have hot sex
with your boyfriend before
the tractor finds you.

338 *Choose someone*
on the tube or street
who looks interesting
and follow them
wherever they go.

Sob quietly to the
world's greatest heart-tweakers:

339 'Hello' by Lionel Richie

340 'Sexual Healing' by Marvin Gaye

341 'You're The First, My Last, My Everything' by Barry White

342 'Mad About the Boy' by Dinah Washington

343 'Three Times A Lady' by the Commodores

344 'I'm Not In Love' by 10cc

345 'You Are Everything' by Diana Ross and Marvin Gaye

346 'Lay Lady Lay' by Bob Dylan

347 'How Deep is Your Love' by the Bee Gees

348 'Tonight I Celebrate My Love For You' by Roberta Flack and Peabo Bryson

(349) Dance the dance
of the Seven Veils.
In other words, make him comfy,
turn the lights down,
the music up and

STRIP.

(350) # Learn to salsa.
La Finca, (020) 7837 5387

(351) *Hire a cleaner.*
It will be money well spent.
No more time wasted feeling guilty
about slobbing on the sofa when
your flat is knee-deep in dust.

(352) **Be Steve McQueen in the**
***Thomas Crown Affair* and**

go gliding.
Booker in Wycombe, (01494) 529263

353 *Have a red-hot office romance.*

It will bring a whole new dimension to your working day.

354 Date *three* different men on *consecutive* nights.

355 Have sex with someone whose name you don't know.

356 *Go on a kibbutz.*

This is like adult camp. It's a working holiday in Israel, where you live and work on a farm picking fruit. You're paid pocket money, but your bed and food are provided. It's a good and cheap way of changing your environment, living in a community and meeting people of different nationalities from different walks of life.

Kibbutz Representatives, (020) 8458 9235

357 Take a riding holiday
– even if you don't ride.
It's good to see the world
from another perspective.

Ride World Wide, (01837) 82544

358 Write an
'Outraged from
Surbiton'
letter to a newspaper and
pray it gets printed.

359 Live in the city
if you grew up in the country.
And vice versa.

360 Fall in love with a builder.
They always have
great muscles.

361 *See Madonna in concert.*
She's one of the best performers of our time.

362 Make sure he has *a sense of* humour. If not, forget it.

363 Say, *'Excuse me?* You're confusing me with someone who *gives a shit,'* to some irksome twit.

364 Buy yourself a diamond. No matter how small. *Diamonds* are a girl's best friend.
H Samuel, (020) 7287 0930

365 *Fall in love* with a *poet.*

And make sure he pens lots of ballads about you.

366 **Give some lucky boyfriend a blow job in the back of a black taxi.**

Computer Cab, (020) 7286 0286

367 *Pretend you're in a Haagen Daaz ad.*

Smear chocolate ice cream on him and lick it off. Let him do the same. It's sticky, cold and messy.

But it's got to be done.

368 *Decorate your home* *in bright, garish colours.*
Everyone needs to have done their bathroom a **cobalt blue** and their sitting room a **bubblegum pink** to understand why most people stick to **magnolia**.

369 Watch the sunrise
from the top of Mount Sinai, the cradle of the world.
(If you're lazy, cheat and travel to the summit by camel.)

370 Deep cleanse with a stint of *colonic irrigation.*
Hale Clinic, (020) 7631 0156

371 Learn another language.
Berlitz, (020) 7915 0909

③72 Ice skate
at the Rockefeller Plaza rink
in New York at Christmas.
Rockefeller Centre, (00 1) 212 632 3975

③73 *Learn to cook an un-lumpy white sauce.*

Soothe your inner demons
with some self-help literature:

374 *I'm OK You're OK*
by **Thomas A Harris**

375 *The Road Less Travelled*
by **Scott M Peck**

376 *You can Heal your Life*
by **Louise L Hay**

377 *Emotional Intelligence*
by **Daniel Coleman**

378 *Men are from Mars, Women are from Venus* by **John Gray**

379 *Feel the Fear and Do it Anyway* by **Susan Jeffers**

380 *The Seven Habits of Highly Effective People* by **Stephen R Covey**

381 *Awaken the Giant Within*
by **Anthony Robbins**

382 *Games People Play* by **Eric Berne**

383 *Are You the One for Me?*
by **Barbara De Angelis**

384 Buy flowers from
Colombia Road market
in East London on a Sunday morning.

385 When you've found Mr Right,
imagine being married in a car park
on a rainy Monday morning.
If you can't imagine being blissfully
happy in such a situation,
don't do it.

386 Snog a girlfriend.

387 Learn the lyrics to
'I Will Survive'.
You're going to need them.

388 *Listen to jazz*

at Ronnie Scott's in Soho, London.
Ronnie Scott, (020) 7439 0747

389 Check out the
sex shops
in London's Soho.

390 *Eat a flower.*

And then pray you haven't
poisoned yourself.

391 Put yourself
out big time
for someone.

And don't mind if they don't thank you.

392 Go on a wine course,
so you'll know which bottle
to order in restaurants.
The Wine Education Service, (020) 8423 6338

393 Buy a filofax and
organize your life.
Or a Palm Pilot if you're a techie type.

394 Do volunteer
work for the Samaritans.
The Samaritans Volunteer Line, (020) 7287 0545

395 Join a demonstration
march *for something
you believe in.*

396 *Learn* to play *tennis.*
It's a very useful, sociable skill.

397 Tell him your

favourite
fantasy

and ask him to tell you his.
And then make his dreams
come true a few days later when
he's not expecting it.
(Best get that nurse's uniform ready ...)

398 Take the sleeper train up to
Fort William in Scotland
and then walk through
atmospheric Glen Coe.

399 *Stand either side*
of the time line
at Greenwich Royal Observatory.

400 Take the river boat
from Westminster to Greenwich.
Westminster Passenger Co., (020) 7930 4097;
Thames Cruises, (020) 7930 3373;
Crown River Cruises, (020) 7936 2033

401 Go to a football match – extra points if it's a Cup Final or an England game.

402 *Gawp* at the *Crown Jewels* at the Tower of London.
Tower of London, (020) 7680 9004

403 Throw a fancy dress party. *And make sure you're the belle of the ball.*
Angels Fancy Dress Hire, (020) 7836 5678; www.fancydress.com

404 *Visit Tate Modern.*
Tate Modern, (020) 7401 5120

405 *Buy some porn:* either a magazine or video will do – and then copy what you see.

406 *Buy a fake fur coat.*

407 **Get an**
Indian head massage.
The London Centre of Indian Champissage,
(020) 7609 3590

408 Read some **Marquis de Sade.**
Not too much,
just enough to get the gist.
And then copy everything he's described.

409 Then read the female version,
Histoire d'Ô
also originally written in French:
And then copy everything *she's* described.

410 *Buy something
from auction.*
But keep a cut-off point firmly in mind.
It's easy to get carried away in
the heat of the moment.

411 *Have a pair of shoes made for you.*

412 Give instructions to a younger sister or friend on a sexual technique.

413 *Get your ears pierced.*

414 *Read about a different religion* from the one you were brought up to believe in – or any religion if you weren't.

415 Go on a course of monthly *Clarins prescription facials.*
Debenhams, (020) 7499 2108; Dickins & Jones, (020) 7434 1766; or phone Clarins head office for your nearest store, (020) 7307 6700

416

Go to a
rubber/bondage party.

417 *Work out if he **intellectualizes emotions** or whether he's empathetic and **right there** with you in **everything** you're feeling.*

The lack of empathy won't be a problem if you intellectualize emotional situations too, but if you're more touchy-feely, it might cause a rift ...

418 *Get an AIDS test.*

**Contact your doctor's surgery or
The Jefferiss Wing, St Mary's Hospital,
Paddington, (020) 7886 1697
for the number of a local STD clinic**

419 *Go to a restaurant and*
eat on your own.

If you're nervous about this, do it
in Paris where eating *toute seule*
means you get the most fabulous
amount of attention from the waiters
and don't really feel alone at all.

420 Don't look on your single
years as a stopgap.
Enjoy them.
Celebrate the freedom.

You'll never be able to be this selfish
once you're married or have kids.

421 *Get medical insurance.*
PPP, 01892 512345 or BUPA, 0800 600500

422 Be away from him
for at least two weeks.
Do you miss him?
If not, is the bond between you strong enough?

423 **Ask yourself this:**
Are you compromising
in any way?
**For instance, you like the
security but don't really fancy him …
If so, forget the wedding.**
No need to compromise until you're at least 40.

424 **Ask yourself this:**
Is your life in a period of flux?
**Are you meeting lots of attractive
eligible men and finding this unsettling?**
If so, put off the wedding for a while.

425 *Have a holiday romance.*

426 **Ask yourself this:**
Imagine marriage is banned.
Do you still want to be with him?

427 **Ask yourself this:**
Are you getting married to please
someone other than yourself
– your mother, for example?
If so, say 'no'.

428 *Watch a foreign film*
without reading the subtitles.
See how much you understand.

429 Gaze enigmatically at the
Mona Lisa
in the Louvre in Paris.

430 *Holiday on a small*
Greek island
*with a group
of girlfriends:*

Kos, Skiathos, Patmos, they're all lovely ...

**Greek National Tourist Organization,
(020) 7734 5997**

431 Buy something
from the internet.

(Check that it's a secure site before you do ...)

Try these ten great sites:

www.thebestofbritish.com (fashion)
www.barclaysquare.co.uk (shopping mall)
www.intofashion.com (fashion)
www.tops.co.uk (fashion)
www.amazon.co.uk (books, videos, music)
www.shopsonthenet.com (everything)
www.shopsmart.com (everything)
www.lobster.co.uk (luxury food items)
www.allwrappedup.co.uk (gifts)
www.flowerservice.co.uk (flowers)

432 Be a selfless matchmaker
and set your
closest girlfriend up with
someone great.

433 Go to the *Isle of Wight*
for the weekend.

434 **Give up wheat for a week**
(pasta, bread, crisps, cakes)
and see how you feel.

435 Try the Eat Right for
your Blood Type diet.
*It worked for Liz Hurley
and Martine McCutcheon,*
so why shouldn't it work for you?

436 *Have a brush with death*
– it can be *someone else's*, it doesn't
have to be *your own* – and get a good
perspective on life and how short it is.

437 Spend Valentine's evening
alone,
and be happy about it.

438 # Go on a pottery course.
*Then make something embarrassing
that you can hide in a cupboard at home.*

439 # *Learn to swim*
if you can't already, and if you can,
swim regularly.
Swimming is an excellent aerobic
exercise that destresses the mind
and works all the muscles you
can't normally get at.

440 ***Hire a barge and holiday
along Britain's canals.***
UK Waterway Holidays, (01992) 550616.

441 *Pretend you're the Empress Poppaea,*
Nero's wife, and bathe in milk.
It's meant to be wonderfully
nourishing for the skin,
leaving it soft and creamy.

442 Get a pedicure.
Do as they do in La-La Land
and make it a regular fixture.

Kitten heels and cracked heels do not go.

**Contact Scarlet head office for
a branch near you, (020) 7581 3602**

443 *Drop* everything
if your friends need you.

444 Spend a day being
completely honest.
See how hard it is.

445 *Floss regularly.*
You know you should.

446 Buy a dildo.
Make it *big*
and *black*.

447 **If you're not sure,**
don't do it.
**Your life doesn't depend on marriage
the way your grandmother's did.**

448 Pay off your overdraft
and clear your credit card bills.
*Don't make the mistake of running
them up again once you're out of the red.*

449 Buy some
strappy stilettos from
Manolo Blahnik
and wave goodbye to £300.

Manolo Blahnik, (020) 7352 3863

450 **Go to the cinema on your own.**

451 *Enjoy breakfast on your own* **on Saturday or Sunday mornings.**

452 Be your *grandmother* for a day and *wash* your *hair* in natural ingredients:

two eggs and a tablespoon of rum. Use warm water, not hot, or the eggs will coagulate.

453 Watch *Four Weddings and a Funeral* with girlfriends.

454 *Knit a scarf.* *Knitting may sound old maidish, but it's incredibly therapeutic.*

455 *Give up bitching/gossiping for a week and see how much better you feel.*

456 **Stand up to your parents** – leave home.

457 Go through a phase of buying only *second-hand clothes.* *Make sure you dry-clean or wash them thoroughly once you get them home.*

458 **Find the right job for you.** *Discover your vocation.*

459 Invest in a good body brush and scrub away that cellulite.

460 *Don't* take his love for granted

– a ring doesn't guarantee lifelong adoration.

461 Talk money

– if you're going to share your life together don't avoid difficult conversations about how you're going to merge your finances.

462 If you're getting **bored** with your sex life and need to go really weird, copy Howard Stern and get yourselves *a blow-up doll.*

Watch your boyfriend have sex with her (it?).
www.realdoll.com

463 *Get into homeopathy.*

Getting antibiotics from the doctor is not always the healthiest way to go. Alternative medicine is just as powerful in certain cases.

Contact the British Homeopathic Association for information on practitioners near you, (020) 7935 2163 or www.nhsconfed.org/bha

464 Move into a *hotel* for a week –
when you're not on holiday.

465 Shave your pubes off
for *heightened* pleasure;
but be prepared for *the itch*
as they grow back.

466 *Trek* to the top of
Machu Picchu in Peru.

467 Learn to fall in love
without losing yourself.

Infatuation won't last, strong healthy love will:
it may change forms but it will endure.

468 Come to terms with the fact that
you'll **never** be able to alter
the length of your legs or
the width of your ankles.

469 Trek to the continental divide in the Rocky Mountains in New Mexico.

The view is stunning.

470 *Kiss* under the Bridge of Sighs *in Venice.*

471 Visit Cuba *before Castro dies* and it turns into an American themed play-park.

472 *Introduce yourself*
to a good-looker at a party
with the following words:

*'Make sure your name's
written on your heart,
because you're just
about to lose it.'*

473 **Learn to**
spend within
your means.
Don't live a champagne life
on a beer income.
It'll just lead to worry.

474 Have a
shiatsu massage.
**For practitioners near you, contact the
British School of Shiatsu, (020) 7281 1412
or www.shiatsuplace.com**

Memorize at least one line
from the world's greatest love films:

475 *Love Story* **starring Ali McGraw and Ryan O'Neal** – have a box of hankies ready

476 *When Harry Met Sally* **starring Meg Ryan and Billy Crystal**

477 *Casablanca* **starring Humphrey Bogart and Lauren Bacall** – cry a lot

478 *The Philadelphia Story* **starring Katharine Hepburn and Cary Grant**

479 *Brief Encounter* **starring Celia Johnson and Trevor Howard**

480 *Out of Africa* **starring Meryl Streep and Robert Redford**

481 *Doctor Zhivago* – marvel at how beautiful Julie Christie is

482 *The Bridges of Madison County* **starring Meryl Streep and Clint Eastwood**

483 *Green Card* **starring Gerard Depardieu and Andie McDowell**

484 *The English Patient* **starring Ralph Fiennes and Kristen Scott Thomas**

485 *Climb a munro.*

These are hills of over 900 m/3,000 ft.
(There are about 300 of them in the UK).

486 *Swim in a pool of balloons.*

487 Hire a limo

and schmooze around town
for the night with a
bunch of rowdy girlfriends.

488 *Wave him goodbye with the words:*
'Give me a call
when you go
through evolution.'

489 *Talk to a psychic.*

And then realize *you* have to take
responsibility for your own life
and not *expect* others to tell you
it's *going* to be OK.

490 Watch Jerry Springer
– and be aware of just how nasty
things might get later ...

491 Go *skinny*
dipping in the sea
– and not just at midnight.

492 Go to *Mardi Gras*
somewhere in the world:
New Orleans, Venice, Sydney ...

493 Go on a blind date.

494 *Take some
singing lessons.*
*Even if you can't sing, they teach you how to
breathe properly and are very therapeutic.*

495 Kiss in a (working)
fountain.

496 Go clubbing
all night
and stick it out through the next day chill-out party, too.

497 Get your hair
permed.
Not too tight though.
You don't have to look like
Kevin Keegan in the 1970s.
There are loose waves, spiral curls,
ringlets, demi-waves and
plenty more to choose from.

498 *When you've found The One,*
check out the in-laws.
*Particularly your mother-in-law.
Ensure she won't be too intrusive in your lives.*

499 **When you think
you've found Mr Right,**
have a *good look around*
to be absolutely sure he is The One.

500 Spend a night in a
haunted house.
Try the Presidential Suite in the
Mansions Hotel in San Francisco if
you can't think of anywhere closer to home.
The Mansions Hotel, (00 1) 800 826 9398

501 *Write some graffiti*
on the door of a public ladies' loo.

502 *Learn three magician's tricks*
*and be the favourite entertainer
at a children's birthday party.*

503 *Smooth*
that furrowed brow
with a spot of Botox. It paralyses the
muscles that allow you to frown,
making you look less tired,
calmer and more serene.
Harley Medical Group, (020) 7631 5494

504 # Kiss at the top of a big wheel.
(Brighton Pier and Blackpool have huge ones.)

505 Seriously consider liposuction.

And then love yourself as you are.

506 Take a **picnic** to Richmond Deer Park.

507 Listen to the Festival of Nine Lessons and Carols sung by the King's Choir at King's College, Cambridge on Christmas Eve.

King's College, Cambridge, (01223) 331100

508 Do a ton
(drive a hundred miles an hour)
in a sports car.

509 Beat a boy at pool.

(He'll hate it but grudgingly admire you.)

510 Have an *affair* with an older man.

(Just to see whether experience makes for a better bed fellow.)

511 Clean out your lungs and *angst* with the occasional Tarzan yell.

For best results, do it in public.

512 Is he easy-going or is he judgemental?

Does he let the day happen as it comes or does he have a rigorous schedule with lists of things to do?

If he's the latter, will he turn his judgemental attitude onto you when the honeymoon period is over?

Can you deal with it if this is the case?

513 Dance at La Escuelita

– a Puerto Rican transvestite night club – in New York.

La Escuelita, 301 West 39th, corner of 8th

514 Have sex in the back of a car.

It's very uncomfortable and you'll soon learn not to do it again.

515 Invest in some shares.

(But not too many, so that if they go down you're not left on the streets looking for breakfast.)

516 Walk through the beautiful bluebell woods of the Birks in Dunkeld, Scotland.

517 Learn to recognize a *beech*, oak, *chestnut,* cedar and elm tree.

You don't have to hug them to appreciate nature.

518 Take a **three-month** sabbatical from **work** and

do something you've always wanted to do.

519 *Try Pilates*

– it's very good for the **posture** and for **strengthening** and stretching your **limbs**. Back sufferers claim it works **wonders**.

Body Control Pilates Information Line, 0870 1690000

520 Enjoy gracious living

with a short stay at the Certosa di Maggiano
in Siena in Italy. This former fourteenth-century
monastery has stunning gardens.

Certosa di Maggiano, (00 39) 5 77 288 180

521 Get tested
for Clamydia.

*(You won't know if you have it
but it can leave you sterile.)*

**Contact your doctor's surgery
or The Jefferiss Wing, St Mary's Hospital,
Paddington, (020) 7886 1697
for the number of a local STD clinic**

522 Snog a best man at a wedding.

523 See the lions
at Longleat, Wiltshire.

Longleat, (01985) 844400

524 Pretend you're
Christine Keeler
and *frolic* in the pool
at Cliveden in Berkshire.

*If you can't get there, strip, turn your chair
around and assume the classic Keeler pose.*

Cliveden House Hotel, (01628) 668561

525 Make a speech:
at a wedding, meeting, or impromptu
party. Know that if needs be,
you can speak publicly.

526 *Sleep with a man of a different race.*

527 Give up coffee
for a week.
And see if you're able to stay
awake naturally.

528 Detox one weekend at Champneys.

Champneys, (01442) 291000

529 *Stroll through the Place des Vosges* in le Marais in Paris.

It's where Victor Hugo lived and is stunningly elegant.

530 Have a relationship where you don't play any games.

It's **by far** the healthiest way.

(And you'll probably end up marrying him.)

531 Give up the sun

and use fake tan instead. Celebs love St Tropez tan, available from Fenwick in Bond Street.

Fenwick, (020) 7629 9161

532 Take the Staten Island ferry
from # Manhattan.

533 *Get your legs
waxed regularly.*

(Shaving leaves them much rougher and stubblier.)

534 Be a **waitress** for an evening.
(And realize how important it is to be polite when ordering food yourself.)

535 *Attend* a *wedding abroad*.
(And be sure that if you do the same, the venue you choose is beautiful enough to warrant your friends traipsing there for you.)

536 Flick through
Homes & Gardens
and *Elle Decoration*
with him to see if you both want to live in the same sort of home.

537 *See the sunset*
from Raleigh Beach, Krabi, Thailand. A bigger apricot sunset you are unlikely to see anywhere else on earth.

538 Spend an entire day watching TV.

539 Bake a **friend** a *birthday* cake.

540 Finish with him in style. Say: *'Don't take this the wrong way, but go right away.'*

541 Go out on a **first** date on a Friday night

and end up crawling home late on Sunday evening.

542 Wake up in someone else's bed, **God knows where,** with a God-forsaken hangover, no make-up remover or clean pants **and a** meeting at 9 am with an important client.

543 Eat at the
Jules Verne Restaurant
at the top of the
Eiffel Tower.

(But book – and save money – well in advance.)

It's one of the best restaurants in Paris.
Jules Verne, (00 33) 1 45 55 61 44

544 Be **featured** in a story in the **papers.**

(Your industry press counts, too …)

Boogie your heart out to the best disco anthems ever:

545 *'We Are Family'* **by Sister Sledge**

546 *'Le Freak'* **by Chic**

547 *'Night Fever'* **by the Bee Gees**

548 *'Stayin' Alive'* **by the Bee Gees**

549 *'I Feel Love'* **by Donna Summer**

550 *'I Will Survive'* **by Gloria Gaynor**

551 *'Don't Stop Til You Get Enough'* **by Michael Jackson**

552 *'YMCA'* **by Village People** – and make sure you do the arm actions

553 *'I Don't Believe (Oops Up Side)'* **by The Gap Band**

554 *'Boogie Wonderland'* **by Earth, Wind and Fire**

555 Try a sensitive type.

Remember Zsa Zsa Gabor's advice:

'*Macho does not mean mucho.'*

556 Avenge yourself on a double-crossing boyfriend:

buy a juicer, invite him over and make him a cucumber and pear drink.

He'll have uncontrollable wind for the next two days.

(Never combine fruit and vegetable juices unless they're apple or carrot.)

557 Be completely *computer* literate.

Go on a course if you have to.

558 Try Dr Atkins's
New Diet Revolution.

This is a very low carb diet, aiming to regulate insulin which results in less fat storage and fewer food cravings.

559 Gate-crash a celebrity party.

560 *Get back* money *from anyone who owes you.*

561 Visit the **red light** district of Patpong in Bangkok.

(Back at your hotel, impress your boyfriend with a few new tricks, as demonstrated by the girls at the bar …)

562 Get into aromatherapy,

the ancient practice of using the essential
oils of certain plants in medicines,
spices and perfumery. Lavender helps you
to relax and sleep, clary sage is an
uplifting antidepressant and eucalyptus is
an insect repellent that helps to
relieve muscle aches and pains.

There is a plethora of delicious
aromas out there waiting
to fill your living space.

**Aromatherapy Organizations Council, (020) 8251 7912
or www.aromatherapyassociates.com
or www.aroma-therapeutics.com
or www.tisserand.com**

563 Contact estranged
members of your family.
Try and work it out.

564 Have a good laugh:
read *A Confederacy of Dunces.*
by John Kennedy Toole.

565 Have sex in the
'rent by the hour'
rooms in Bangkok airport.

566 Make a list of 20 things you'd
like your ideal man to have:
i.e. good looks,
sense of humour,
tight buns, etc.,
and compare your list with the
real thing. This way you'll know if
he's on the right lines or not.

567 Practise a little S&M
and use handcuffs in bed.

568 *Play strip poker.*

569 Locate your
G-spot.

(Named after the German doctor,
Grafenberg, who identified it, it's
about the size of a 10p piece
and can usually be found on the front
vaginal wall, a couple of centimetres up.)

570 Locate his
G-spot.

(Prepare yourself.
It's probably somewhere
up his bum. *Eyuw.*)

571 Make sure he can *bring* you to orgasm.

572 *Talk dirty with him.*

And watch his reaction. If he's horrified, prepare yourself for a relationship of repression …

573 Have a French manicure.

(The one where they paint the tips white and the rest of the nail a natural colour. Very elegant, very soigné …)

Contact Scarlet head office for a local branch, (020) 7581 3602

574 Pretend you're *Audrey*.

Wearing diamonds and a black
Givenchy evening gown, eat a danish
while gazing in the windows
of Tiffany's in New York at 6 am.

575 Learn to tell a **joke** properly – one that'll have him rolling in the aisles (and then up it, too).

576 Give blood.

577 *Try a Brazilian wax* – all the girls in New York do it.

(Warning: it's painful: they wax everything apart from a nodule above the *mons Veneris*. Behind, between, around …)

578 Be an adult bridesmaid. Experience the humiliation and then vow never to put your friends through that.

579 Play **bingo** at your local leisure centre.

580 Locate the **Plough** and the **Great Bear** *in the summer night sky.*

581 Experience the lifestyle of *the super-rich* by visiting Hearst Castle in San Simeon, California.

Hearst Castle, (00 1) 805 927 2020

582 Change jobs at least once.

583 *Nurse someone through an illness.*
It does not have to be life-threatening – flu will do, but you'd better brush up on your Florence Nightingale skills. Men tend to need a lot of cosseting when they're ill.

584 Go to the Edinburgh Festival one August and see **five plays** in a day.

585 Eat at Rick Stein's
Seafood Restaurant
in Padstow, Cornwall.
The Seafood Restaurant, (01841) 532700

586 *Enjoy a New Year's Eve,*
even when single.
Especially when single!

587 Work out how compatible you are.
You can tell a lot about a man
by his sleeping patterns:

Does he spoon you? **(Good sign if he does.)**

Does he let you spoon him? **(Ditto.)**

Does he sleep facing away from you
on the edge of the bed?
**(Bad sign: signifies he has difficulty
revealing his emotions.)**

Does he insist on no touching during
the night? **(Bad sign: he could be repressed.)**

588 *Enjoy the all-night light and wallow in the cloudy blue mineral-rich waters of the Blue Lagoon outside Reykjavik in Iceland in the summer.*

589 If you're feeling low, go and have an Andrew & Liz Collinge

complete makeover at Harrods.

This includes a haircut by Andrew, a champagne lunch, a manicure and advice on a new image.

Harrods Ladies Hair & Beauty Salon, (020) 7893 8333

590 Persuade the pilot to let you up onto the flight deck

to while away the time while flying long haul.

591 Attend a funeral.

592 Have
champagne
for breakfast –
*preferably in bed and brought
to you by someone else.*

593 Know how to cook
a Sunday roast.

594 Apply to be a contestant on
Cilla Black's
Blind Date.

595 Have sex in a lift.
**(Make sure the building's tall, or it
could get embarrassing.)**

596 Know how to mix a good **cocktail** –

something more complicated than a gin and tonic though: a Bellini or Margarita, for instance. (If you need to watch the professionals go to Jonathan Downey's Match Bar in London, or if you're feeling really flush get the staff with their portable bar and drinks cabinet to come to you.)

Match Bar, Margaret Street, W1, (020) 7499 3443, www.matchbar.com

597 For a nostalgic afternoon, go to a British seaside resort out of season –

Eastbourne, for example.

598 Face oblivion:

drop 60 m (200 ft) in two seconds on the Oblivion ride at Alton Towers.

Alton Towers, 0870 5204060

599 Go on an Italian **cookery** course.

Try Alastair Little's fabulous culinary weeks in Tuscany and Umbria.
Tasting Places, (020) 7460 0077

600 *Pretend you're The Rock*
and say to someone who's pissing you off:

'Why don't you go into the kitchen, open the fridge, take out the carton and pour yourself a nice long cool drink of SHUT UP juice ...'

(Be cool and slow in your delivery, but SHOUT the 'shut up' part.)

601 Meet an **astronaut.**

602 Cook a *soufflé.*

They're not as difficult as you think.

(Just copy Delia word for word.)

603 Go to **Hatton Cross**
on the Piccadilly Line
*and watch the jumbos heading for
Heathrow just a few metres above your head.*

604 Watch Parliamentary Question
Time from the Visitors' Gallery
in the House of Commons.

The House of Commons, (020) 7219 3000

605 Spend *Saturday*
afternoon pedaloing on
the *Serpentine.*

606 Get your overalls on and
help a friend paint
their new home.

607 Buy a vibrator. Introduce him to it.

608 *Try an Eve Lom facial*

(and wave goodbye to a hundred quid ...)

Eve Lom is a cleansing guru. Her facials involve paraffin wax, which softens the skin and opens the pores ready for deep extraction of blackheads and other nasties. Facials also include a massage of the neck and shoulders.

Eve Lom Salon & Skincare Product Enquiries, (020) 7935 9988 or www.evelom.co.uk

609 Give other diners a thrill: wear large, black *Jackie O* glasses in a restaurant and refuse to take them off.

By the time you leave they'll all be wondering who you are.

610 Attend an opening night
(art gallery, theatre, opera, for instance.)

611 Go through a
vitamin phase

and eat a plethora of pills for breakfast.
(Watch your pee turn yellow-green later.)

612 *Buy yourself a leather jacket.*
(And pretend you're the Fonz.)

613 Check out his lifestyle habits:

Is he dirty and messy?
Does he expect someone to tidy
up after him?
*Or is he maniacally tidy and you're the
opposite?* Can you live with that?

Work it out, now. Living together will
bring such differences to the fore,
and you need to be sure you can handle it.

614 *Be bossy for a day.*
(Or be meek if you're bossy already.)

Be well read. Try these modern classics:

615 *Captain Corelli's Mandolin*
by Louis de Bernières

616 **Mug up on philosophy with**
Sophie's World **by Jostein Gaarder**

617 *Animal Farm* **by George Orwell**
– and realize that we're not all equal

618 *The Great Gatsby*
by F Scott Fitzgerald

619 *Wild Swans* **by Jung Chang**

620 *Brideshead Revisited*
by Evelyn Waugh

621 *Beloved* **by Toni Morrison**

622 *Love in the Time of Cholera*
by Gabriel García Márquez

623 *Lucky Jim* **by Kingsley Amis**
– for a good laugh

624 *Zen and the Art of Motorcycle
Maintenance* **by Robert M Pirsig**

625 Be interviewed

for something other than a job.
(By a journalist for an article is
fine, but the police count too …)

626 Greet him when he
comes home from work
dressed up like a
St Trinian's
school girl
with a whip in your hand.

627 Serve *pink
champagne* at dinner.

628 Go to Angkor Wat in Cambodia
and be awe-inspired by the stunning Khmer ruins.

629 Have sex on the kitchen table
– at his parents' home.
Or, if you're feeling really brave, do it in
their bed for that naughty teenage thrill.

630 Watch the sunset over the **River Arno**
from the Ponte Vecchio in Florence.

631 **Buy an expensive watch:**
Cartier, Longines, Rolex ...

632 Sleigh ride through the snow
in St Petersburg.

(Wrap up in real fur
it's the only thing
that'll keep you warm.)

633 Shoot a gun.
(Try a funfair if you don't have any friends in the army.)

634 Ride *white horses* in the Camargue
and stay at Le Mas du Peint, near Arles,
where the food is exceptional.

Le Mas du Peint, (00 33) 4 90 97 20 62

635 Get onto a film set.
**Or if all else fails, visit Universal Studios
in Hollywood. Universal Studios,
(00 1) 818 622 3801**

636 Get *upgraded* to first class when flying.
(Always dress smartly, and always ASK.)

637 *Keep a secret.*

638 Suggest a romantic week at the Ladera resort in **St Lucia** *(and pray that he pays).*

The point of Ladera is that the rooms are all missing their fourth wall, so you sleep almost under the stars, with a view of the sea and the Grand and Petit Pitons, St Lucia's beautiful mountains.

Call Seasons in Style, (0151) 3420505

639 *Vote* in a general election.

640 *Don't be scared of your anger.* Use it and realize it's **energy.**

641 Visit the stunning Moorish Alhambra palace in Granada.

(Drive through the Granada pass to get there.)

642 Have a *proper* conversation with a star.

(Something other than just asking for their autograph.)

643 *Ski the* Vallée Blanche *in Chamonix, France.*

644 Get a full-body scrub in a Hammam.

(They're all over the Arab countries – and there are a few in Paris, too.)

645 Stay on a houseboat at the *Acacia Hotel* in Amsterdam.
Acacia Hotel, (00 31) 20 62 21 460

646 Take a helicopter ride.
Cab Air, (020) 8953 4411 or
Biggin Hill Helicopters, (01959) 540803

647 Celebrate the solstice, June 21st, at Stonehenge.
Stonehenge Stone Circle, (01980) 624715

648 *Steal a fluffy white towelling dressing gown from a flash hotel without their noticing.*

649 Give money to charity.

650 Dive off the Great Barrier Reef
in Australia.

651 **Another great way to
get rid of an idiot:**
just say, 'Don't let the doorknob hit
you in the arse on the way out.'

652 *Try Prozac.*

653 Have anal sex.
(Do **NOT** have normal sex afterwards
until you've washed ...)

654 **Experience total luxury:**
stay at the Regent Resort in Chiang Mai.
The Regent Chiang Mai Resort and Spa,
(00 66) 53 298 181

655 See a *bullfight* in Spain.
(Then date the torreador.)

656 Down a pint in one.
(Try not to throw up afterwards.)

657 Go to *Sunsplash*
– the Reggae Festival in Jamaica.
Sunsplash information
www.cwjamaica.com/reggaesun

658 **Give yourself a home-made facial:**

clean your face with egg yolk (it'll be very
silky as well as very clean afterwards), rinse with
rose-water and then apply a base cream
of half a pot of yogurt beaten with a
couple of drops of almond oil.

659 *Study the*
Kama Sutra *closely.*

660 Ride with
cowboys
in Texas.

Yee haw.

661 Buy a handbag from Gucci.
And expect to pay a minimum of £300.
Gucci, (020) 7629 2716

662 Be Sue Ellen
from *Dallas* for a night.
Throw a drink in a rude man's face.

663 *Leave an objectionable date
halfway through the meal.*
Walk out of the restaurant
and revel in your boldness.

664 Drink Guinness
in the Temple Bar district
in Dublin.
Irish Tourist Board Information, 0800 0397000

665 *Save electricity.*
Use candlelight only for an entire weekend at
home. Everything will look nicer – including you.

666 Learn to say 'no'.

667 Keep him *quiet.*
Say, *'Next time you want to share your stupidity, just keep it a secret.'*

668 Be environmentally aware.

Cycle to work one week in the summer (or walk if it's possible – i.e. anything up to an hour's walk away).

669 Buy a Toby Mott logo T-shirt – *'I must stop snogging the boys,'* for instance or *'I hate work.'*

Call Toby Mott for your nearest stockist, (020) 7727 7244

670 Love and worship Top Shop.
It's the best place for up-to-the-minute affordable hip-chick gear.

671 Enjoy the incredible view of Rome through the keyhole of the garden gate at the Knights of Malta (Piazza Cavalieri di Malta) on the Aventine Hill.

672 *Before you leave your* *single days behind,* *remember what Joan Rivers said:*

'Trust your husband, adore your husband. And get as much as you can in your own name.'

673 Get plenty of sleep.
If it's not the sex it'll be the kids that keep you awake later on. Try to be in bed by 10 pm and asleep by 10.30 pm one night a week.

674 Play *drinking games* with friends.

Try this one: have a *conversation* where every *thing you say* is a question. Anyone who *replies* without asking a question has to *drink*.

675 *Get into the habit of writing lists.*

Far from **intimidating** you with what you have to do, **lists** can also be **used** to make you feel **good**: for instance, write a list of what you've achieved **today**. Also, write a list of your **future** plans, put it **away** somewhere and look at it **now** and **then**.

Are you on track?

676 *Detox* thoroughly: have a lymph drainage massage and clear out your waste disposal system. Read Leslie Kenton's *The Cellulite Revolution,* the ultimate guide to detoxifying.

677 Be in control of your
emotions in a
relationship; don't let
them run you.

If you are feeling 'flooded' step outside yourself and realize that this moment will pass, that you have experienced something similar before and will do so again, **and that you can TAKE IT.**

678 *Join the army.*
**The Army Career Information Line,
(08457) 300111**

679 Gorge on the food of love
and treat him to the erotic banquet at
Castle Leslie in Dublin.
Castle Leslie, (00 353) 47 88 109

680 Learn the names of *all the*
cabinet ministers, and their shadows.

681 Try a different form of exercise: spinning for cardiovascular fitness. *It's exhausting, but you'll be incredibly fit after regular sessions.*

682 Spend a Saturday afternoon *flying a kite* on a hill in your local park.

683 Compile a tape or CD of all your favourite songs *and listen to it when you're down for an instant pick-me-up.*

684 *Write a sexy story* and submit it to an **erotic** magazine. Use a **pseudonym** if you're feeling shy.

Empower yourself
with a hip-chick-with-attitude flick:

685 *Thelma and Louise*
starring Susan Sarandon and Geena Davis

686 *Working Girl* **starring Melanie Griffith**

687 *The Last Seduction*
starring Linda Fiorentino

688 *Erin Brockovich* **starring Julia Roberts**

689 *Barbarella* **starring Jane Fonda**

690 *Charlie's Angels*
starring Cameron Diaz and Drew Barrymore

691 *Chacun cherche son Chat*
starring Garrance Clavel

692 *The Bitch* **starring Joan Collins**

693 *Muriel's Wedding*
starring Toni Collette

694 *Wish you were Here*
starring Emily Lloyd

695 Buy some **sexy** underwear from Frederick's of **Hollywood** on Hollywood Boulevard and *flounce* around in it in front of your *loved* one.

Frederick's, (00 1) 323 466 8506

696 Do *The Times* crossword. (That means finish it. You can cheat and do it with someone else if you get stuck.)

697 Read your horoscope in every paper or magazine you come across over the course of a week and see if any of it comes true. *Or get a personal reading from a psychic or tarot card reader.*

698 *Live on a houseboat for a while.*

699 Buy a hamper from Fortnum and Mason, drive out to the country and eat in the grounds of a stately home that's open to the public.

Fortnum and Mason, (020) 7734 8040

700 Queue up
for the opening of the
Harrods Sale.

Harrods, (020) 7730 1234

701 Learn to put a condom on with
your mouth.

702 Tell someone at work that they have BO/halitosis **without** insulting them horribly.

This is a lesson in diplomacy.

703 Become an excellent *kisser*.

(No pointy tongues, no sucking too hard, open mouth ...)

704 See Monet's *Waterlilies* at the Musée d'Orsay in Paris.

Musée d'Orsay, (00 33) 1 40 49 48 14

705 Buy some K-Y jelly and know how, when and why to use it.

(706) Eat as many

oysters

as you can in one sitting.

Scott's in Mount Street, W1, (020) 7629 5248

707 *Buy a good camera*
and take some arty pictures
– ie not the ceiling or your friends
with half their heads chopped off.
Then compile them in a photo album.

708 Shop till you drop
in Bloomingdales on Third Avenue in
New York, so you can swing one of those
'little brown bags' like a true American.
Bloomingdales, (00 1) 212 355 5900

709 *Learn how to download
software from the Internet
onto your computer.*

710 *Buy something from a
mail order catalogue.*
(You might be doing a lot more of this once you
have children and no more time.) Boden,
and LaRedoute are both excellent.
Boden, (020) 453 1535; LaRedoute 0500 777777

711 *Smoke a cigar.*
(You're not meant to inhale,
      but taste it at the back of the throat.)

712 Give up a Christmas
day to work in a
SOUP kitchen.
Homeless Network Limited, (020) 7799 2404

713 *Take your nieces/nephews/friend's children to Hamleys on Regent Street in London for the day.*
(Avoid half term if possible.)
Hamleys, (020) 7494 2000

714 Buy expensive suitcases
and *travel in style.*
Choose Louis Vuitton if you can afford it.
Louis Vuitton, (020) 7399 4050

715 Spend Sunday morning doing a
large and complicated
jigsaw puzzle.

This is an exercise in patience –
something you'll need a lot of later.

716 Create your
own *potpourri*.

Mix the following in a bowl: **flower petals** of
different colours, two **cinnamon sticks**,
50 g each of **mint, rosemary** and **lemongrass**,
7.5 ml of **ground nutmeg**, 7.5 ml of
whole cloves, one **vanilla pod** and three
drops of **lavender oil**.

717 Learn how to cook a really
good fry-up for

hungover Saturday mornings: sausage,
bacon, eggs, tomatoes, mushrooms,
baked beans, toast, the works.

718 *Eat lots of garlic.*

It's good for the heart, builds up your immune system and helps detoxify the blood.

Only thing is, you have to do this while you're single because it makes you a bit stinky – unless you opt for the capsules, of course.

719 Spend an entire day *smiling* at people.

See if all that positive energy does you any good.

720 Ban trashy media for a week:

that means no Hello!-style magazines, no soap operas, no celebrity gossip websites. See what else you can do with your time and mind, instead.

721 Go on a date without any *underwear* on.
Or meet someone from the airport wearing just a raincoat and stilettos.

722 *Become a godparent.*
Whether you're asked or not is a good indicator of how good a friend, and how responsible, you are.

723 Buy a friend a
wedding present
they actually like that's
not from their list.

724 Buy a *large* map of the world.
Maps make excellent artwork for your walls and are great for daydream travel when you're frustrated at work.

725 Go mad – in a good way. *Smash plates in a Greek restaurant.*

726 Learn to
love change.

727 **Bank some sperm**
from a good-looking gay friend.

728 Check out his bank statements
and general credit situation.

*Is he the type to live off an enormous
overdraft? Can you deal with that? Are you
the same or do you need someone
who controls their finances the same way
you do? Work this out so as to
avoid money wrangles in the future.*

729 *Get him to test for HIV.*
**Contact your doctor's surgery or
The Jefferiss Wing, St Mary's Hospital,
Paddington, (020) 7886 1697
for the number of a local STD clinic**

730 *Resolve never to leave the house again without a bottle of*

Bach's Rescue Remedy

(or failing that a hip flask of gin)

about your person. This will come in more than handy when you bump into your ex and his new squeeze/wife in the supermarket. This is guaranteed to happen when you are queuing to buy an armful of cat food, tampons and whiskey, wearing your oldest clothes and no make-up. By contrast, they have a trolley full of healthy, balanced meals and organic crisps.

731 *Buy a Magimix*

and learn to make purées and delicious smooth sauces.

732 Get some handwriting analysed.
If you're feeling dubious about him in any way, get his done. If not, do the people who work for you at the office. It's fascinating and very accurate.

733 Go to a lap-dancing *club in Soho.*

That way you can see what guys get so excited about. And pick up a few tips for when you're entertaining him at home.

734 Crash a stag night.

See what they *really* get up to. It's shocking.

735 Hire a private investigator for a week.

Track someone you've had your doubts about. If it's your potential husband and he's been lying to you, think again HARD.

736 *Get some culture and broaden the mind.*

Go to an exhibition at the Royal Academy of Art in Piccadilly.

Royal Academy of Art, (020) 7300 5760

737 Admit to some
embarrassing
sexual behaviour
to the world at large on
The Graham Norton Show.

738 Learn to give a man his space:
if he's retreating, let him go and wait for him to come back to you. He will if you're cool, confident and don't chase him.

739 *Star spot* while hanging out at the Whiskey Bar at the Sunset Marquis Hotel *in LA.*
Sunset Marquis, (00 1) 310 657 1333

740 Bank a few eggs, just in case you want to postpone having children for a while.

(741) # Rollerblade

**with the other body-beautifuls along
Venice Beach in LA.**

(742) *Wangle a ticket to a fashion
show during Fashion Week.
Choose your city:*

Paris, New York, Milan or London
– and then go to the after-show party.

743 Be open minded about
physical appearances:
go out with someone shorter than
you, or a guy who's balding.
Beauty is in the eye of the beholder, after all ...

744 *Watch the **Oxford** versus **Cambridge**
boat race from the banks of the
Thames, between **Putney** and
Hammersmith bridges, rather than on TV.*

And gamble on it, of course.

745 *Take ballet lessons.*
It will do wonders for your posture.

746 Have your eyebrows
threaded at Harrods.
It lasts longer than waxing or plucking.

**Farida Chaudray at Harrods, (020) 7893 8333
or Vaishaly Patel at Martyn Maxey, (020) 7629 6161**

747 # Don't show him up
in front of his mates.

Behaviour like this is a relationship killer.

748 Enjoy a **mineral-rich** spa under an **original** Ottoman **dome** at the Kiraly **baths** in Budapest.

749 Work out when you need to compromise and when you need to
stamp that nasty habit out.

So ask yourself, what irritates you about him?
If the list is endless, you might
want to think again.

750 Pretend you're **Ernest Hemingway** and drink mojitos *(rum with mint and lime juice)* in La Bodeguita del Medio in Old Havana in Cuba.

751 Work out how compatible you are:
Is he easy-going socially?
Or is he nervous and shy?
Are you embarrassed of
him in any way?
If you are, don't marry him.

752 Go *white-water rafting*
on the island of Reunion.

753 Create your own real
time porn video
*by making love in front of a mirror
while watching yourselves.*

754 And another good use for a mirror:
know thyself.
*Use a mirror to have a good look and
see what you look like down there.*

Buy these excellent CDs:

755 *Big Calm* by Morcheeba

756 *Thriller* by Michael Jackson

757 *Urban Hymns* by The Verve

758 *The Greatest Hits*
by the Rolling Stones

759 *Ray of Light* by Madonna

760 *Here Comes the Sun
and Other Great Hits*
by Nina Simone

761 *Vertigo* by Groove Armada

762 *The All Time Greatest Hits*
by Elvis Presley

763 *Screamadelica* by Primal Scream

764 *40 Greatest Hits* by Diana Ross

765 *Try Moroccan food* –
couscous, kebabs, aubergine spreads … delicious.

766 **Watch the tennis at Wimbledon.**
Wimbledon Lawn Tennis Championships,
(020) 8946 2244

767 Keep endangered species alive:
adopt an animal *in the zoo.*

768 Kiss at the top of the
Eiffel Tower in Paris. Or pretend
you're in *An Affair to Remember* and
kiss at the top of the Empire
State Building in New York.

769 Don't try to change him.
Love him as he is because he will feel unloved
and manipulated if you try to make him different.
Equally, be sure he is not trying to change you.

(770) ## See an opera
in an original language
other than English.
**Royal Opera House in Covent Garden,
(020) 7240 1200 or www.royaloperahouse.org**

(771) Invite all your ex-boyfriends
to dinner at the same time.
Do not invite anyone else.

*Bask in the attention and see if they work
out their connection with each other.*

(772) *Open a secret bank account.*

(773) Buy a bunch of bananas,
get all your girlfriends round,
get drunk and have an
oral sex show-and-tell session.

774 Take a *Thelma and Louise* trip with your best girlfriend, find Brad Pitt but turn around and head back before it all leads to disaster.

775 *Treat him to dinner* at an **expensive** restaurant now and then. Don't **always** expect him to pay for the culinary **treats**.

776 Write him a good love letter. *If you're single, write it to yourself and give yourself a boost.*

777 Climb the lions in Trafalgar Square.

778 Tell an irritant to buzz off. Say: *'Make like a plane and take off.'*

779 Spend an entire day in one of the new New York-style cafés and sample every different type of coffee available: latte, frappuccino, mocca.

780 *Give yourself regular breast examinations. Look out for lumps.*

Early diagnosis is the difference between life and death.

781 Give a **good** blow job.
Be creative. Don't forget his balls.

782 *Learn to row without raising your voice or assigning blame.*
It's hard to do but worth it.
The key to successful relationships is
constructive arguments.
Try and say something nice
to him even when you're angry.

783 *Hear a nightingale sing.*
*(Although these days if you go to
Berkeley Square you might have to
take a tape recording with you ...)*

784 Eat unusual meats:
ostrich, kangaroo or crocodile, for instance.

785 Thank him for favours he does you.
Men love being appreciated.

204 1001 Things You MUST Do Before You Get Married

786 Learn the rudiments of
sign language and have a
conversation with a deaf person.

787 *Hold something back*
right up until you wander down the aisle.

Do not give yourself completely – emotionally or
physically – right away. Make him work for
you or he may feel that what's given too
easily is a) always granted to everyone and
b) not worth much. Harsh, but true.

788 Swim with *manta rays*
in warm water.

789 Don't moan about your
physicality to him: *it's boring.*

*Don't let him know you **hate** your thighs, think the
moon has fewer **craters** than your bum and that
you could **easily** tie your tits behind your ears.
Be **confident** in your body and he'll **love** it, too.*

790 Go on a massage course.

And give your friends and boyfriend a treat.
If you're really good you could even
create another source of
income for yourself.

**Fax the British Massage Therapy Council,
(01772) 881063**

791 Kiss on a *bridge* in the *rain* until you're *soaked* through.

792 Ask yourself this:

*Does he put you down?
Does he make comments like: 'You've put
on a bit of weight' or
'Are you sure you should eat that cream bun?'
Does he make you feel self-conscious
about your body or your personality in any way?*

If the answer is 'yes' to any of these, seriously,
think again. He should make you feel good
about yourself (and vice versa). And if he doesn't,
there will be battles ahead.

793 Be able to identify five pieces of classical music.

Some easy popular pieces are
Beethoven's *Pastoral Symphony*,
Mozart's overture to *The Marriage of Figaro*, Handel's *Arrival of the Queen of Sheba*, Vivaldi's *The Four Seasons* and Tchaikovsky's *Swan Lake*.

794 *Go whale-watching* in Monterey, California.

795 **Don't expect perfection from him.** *You're not going to get it.*

796 Realize that the key to a relationship is *avoiding* dishonesty rather than an *excess* of honesty:

(for instance, when your mum asks if she looks old, you're unlikely to say 'yes' even if she is looking a bit tired ...)

797 *Don't* be a nag.
It's damaging to his self-esteem
and will eventually ruin your sex life.

798 *See the sun rise from a plane.*

799 **Realize that your man is not psychic.**
What may be blindingly obvious to you may
not even have brushed his consciousness yet.

800 *Charm his friends.*

801 Learn to control your temper.
*But also be sure you know the full
extent of his. If he's violent, or shows even a
hint of a tendency towards violence, think
again. It's ugly watching someone
destroy the furniture. And sooner or
later they'll turn on you.*

802 Sponsor a child in Africa.
**Contact Action Aid, (01460) 238000
or World Vision, (01908) 841000**

803 # Don't keep score

in your relationship. It's ungenerous.
If you are keeping tabs the balance is
clearly upset already.

804 ## *Feed the ducks*

in St James' Park in London.

805 If your needs are **not** being met,
don't stop **expressing** them.
*If you do, and start relying on yourself to get
things done, the resentment will only increase.*

806 Spend *one* weekend
in a *grand*
country house.

807 Take a vow of silence for one day.
See if you can do it.

808 **Keep unwanted advice to yourself.**
It implies you think he's
not doing it right.

809 Appreciate and understand
his way of *loving* you.
*It may not be his style to tell you he loves you
every other day, but he may put himself
out to give you a lift to work
when you're not feeling well, for instance.*

810 *Take the **tube** in London
to the **end** of the line.*

811 Take a note of how
he treats animals.
It's a foretaster of how he'll be with the kids.
Do you like what you see?

812 **Let him take you to the rugby at Twickenham**
(or whatever his sport of choice is).
And look like you're having a good time (even if you're not).

813 *Learn how to barbecue meat properly:*
i.e. not burning the outside while leaving the inside raw.

814 Heckle a stand-up comedian.
(Doing it to the telly is cheating. You need to see them live.)

815 Organize an *outing*
for a bunch of girlfriends to see a silly musical like *Mamma Mia* or a sexy one like *Chicago*.

816 Know the storylines and one major aria from the easy operas: ***La Traviata, Carmen* or *Tosca*.**

817 *Apply for the US*
Green card lottery
Then if it all goes wrong you can at least escape to New York permanently.

818 Buy coloured contact lenses and change the colour of your eyes for a day.

819 *Plant a tree.*

820 ***Let him know how you really feel with the words:***
'You have the sort of face only a mother could love so long as she was a potato, too.'

821 *Buy a Montblanc pen.*
Montblanc in Burlington Arcade, W1, (020) 7493 6369 or Royal Exchange, (020) 7929 4200)

822 ***Bathe by candlelight.***

Read *something* light:

823 *Riders* by Jilly Cooper

824 *Hollywood Wives* by Jackie Collins

825 *Marrying the Mistress*
by Joanna Trollope

826 *Bridget Jones's Diary*
by Helen Fielding

827 *The Horse Whisperer*
by Nicholas Evans – the book's much
sexier than the film

828 *Circle of Friends* by Maeve Binchy

829 *Come Together*
by Josie Lloyd and Emlyn Rees

830 *Grand Sophy* by Georgette Heyer

831 *The Firm* by John Grisham

832 *You'll Never Eat Lunch in
this Town Again* by Julia Phillips

833 *Rosie Meadows Regrets*
by Catherine Alliott

834 Learn a few *measuring* techniques and spare yourself the *embarrassment* of being *confronted* with something eeny-weeny: from the end of his *finger* to the palm of his *hand* is the same length as his penis when it's erect.

835 Let him be *friends* with anyone he *wants* – whether male or female.
Easier said than done. Remember, even though jealousy shows that you want each other and find each other sexy, being possessive will soon make him feel manipulated and stifled.

836 *Having said that, keep an eye on any encroaching ex-girlfriends.*
If they're getting too close, draw his attention to the fact. If he's decent he'll make it clear where his priorities lie to both of you. But do this early on in the relationship, while the goodwill between you is still vibrating strongly …

837 *Train yourself:*
don't call him more than *once* a day
at the *office*. He has a job of
work to do – and so do you!

838 Write a poem.

839 **Learn** *to hear him out when he has*
complaints, rather than wading in with
your own view. For a start, he'll soon run
out of rants and secondly, you'll look
super-cool, calm and collected.

840 *Take the initiative.*
Suggest **fun** things to do at the **weekend** or for
your **holidays**. Don't always expect him to
do the **running**. (Although if he never
suggests **anything**, you might want to **consider**
whether he's **dynamic** enough for you.)

841 Buy a blindfold,
put it on him in bed and tease
him erotically all over.
*(If he doesn't go for this, you can always
strap it on yourself in the car if you
find his driving a tad scary.)*

842 Experience other countries'
national holidays:

for instance the 14th July in France or
the 4th July in the USA.

843 *Share a man with a girlfriend.*
(Not necessarily at the same time, but on
the same night and in the same place ...)

844 *Kiss on a
Bateau Mouche
in Paris.*

Bateaux Mouches, (00 33) 1 40 76 99 99

845 *Pretend you're a Texan and try big hair.*

Backcomb till you're blue in the face.

846 Wear *edible* underwear.

Ann Summers order line, (020) 8645 8300

(847) *Spice up your career:*

wear Chinese love balls to work one day
and see if anyone else can hear them
tinkling around inside you.

(But be warned: not all women can feel them.)

(848) Try hydrotherapy.

It's a water treatment that's
particularly good for cellulite because
it works on the circulation.

**General Council and Register of Naturopaths,
(01485) 840072**

(849) *Talking of water works:*

find out where he stands on kinky sex.
Be sure you can deal with all his demands
so as to prevent him looking elsewhere further
down the line. Equally, is he adventurous
enough for you or might your eye start
wandering later on, too?

850 Do you row about the *same* things time and time again?

If so, work out those issues once and for all. **Move on! Ditch the past!**

851 *Take a* *freezing cold* *shower every morning for a week.*

It'll get your energy and circulation going and make you feel more alive.

852 Dress up as a clown *for a friend's child's birthday party.*

853 *Be the best 'you' possible!*

Work towards your dreams. You'll soon discover that they're not as unattainable as they seem.

854 Keep your *sex life* alive.

Try a no-sex **policy** for a few days:
It's **amazing** how **tempting**
forbidden fruits become.

855 Have a quiet moment
and read a book in
New York's public library

**New York Public Library is on
42nd Street between Fifth and
Sixth Avenues, (00 1) 212 340 0849**

856 Don't say it!

Practise biting your lip when nasties bubble
up on your tongue. Courtesy is one of the keys
to a happy relationship. And once you and he
have yelled your heads off at each other,
all those malicious things can't be unsaid.
Best not to say them in the first place.

857 *Buy incredible* cakes *and* cheeses *from Fauchon in Paris, perhaps the world's most* famous *delicatessen.*

Fauchon is off the Place de la Madeleine, (00 33) 1 47 62 60 11

858 **Work out how compatible you are.**

How does he **see** *the world? In terms of lots of* **facts** *or as a* **realm** *of infinite possibilities?*

If it's the latter, will you find him too vague and impossible to pin down or, if the former, too rigid and unromantic? Know where you stand on these questions, too, so that you can take any differing views into account.

859 Drink a bellini

(peach juice and champagne) *in Harry's Bar in Venice.*

Harry's Bar, (00 39) 41 528 5777

860 Learn to read all small print.
Don't rely on lawyers to do this for you.

861 Work out if you want children and, if so, how many.
Find out how he feels about this. If you hate kids and he is dying to hear the sound of tiny feet, you will need to have a serious discussion. In the meantime, buy him a chihuahua.

862 *Be consistent* in all approaches to life, but especially in your relationship. *Consistency breeds trust.*
People know where they are with you. Your employers will give you more responsibility at work, your friends will reciprocate, and your man will respect you.

863 Gallop a horse along the seashore:
the perfect antidote for urban stress.

864 *Ask him if he ever gets cold sores –*
and keep an eye out for them.
Control your passion if/when he has
them and BAN oral sex. Cold sores
are a form of herpes.

865 # Run a marathon.

Train first or you could do yourself
great damage. Too much running
can make your face look drawn
and your limbs feel angry.

The London Marathon, (020) 7620 4117

866 # Experience
super-kitsch luxury

in the Palazzo Versace hotel on
Australia's Gold Coast in Queensland.

Everything in the hotel is by Versace – and for sale.

**Qantas Holidays, (020) 8222 9104;
Palazzo Versace, (00 61) 7 55 09 80 00**

867 Buy one of the world's most
sophisticated and elegant handbags:
the Kelly bag made famous by Grace Kelly.
But be prepared – there's a waiting list.
Hèrmes, (020) 7499 8856

868 Buy some **foreign** footwear:
espadrilles, **clogs,** moccasins …

869 # Perform.
Whether it's with a **local choir** or in amateur dramatics, get out there and **show** your **face**. See what it's like to be **stared** at by countless others.

870 Let him see you looking frumpy:

no make-up, tired, unglamorous.
If he's critical, think again. You're
unlikely to look like Julia Roberts when
you're changing the kids' nappies later on.

871 Be a DJ on hospital radio.

*Cheer up the lonely and unwell by
playing them some groovy tunes.*

872 *Be a groupie.*

Hang out at stage doors.

873 Learn to trust yourself
and your instincts.

They will **always** tell you the way you
need to go – even if it **sometimes** seems
to be up the **garden path**; after all,
valuable lessons come from mistakes.

874 *Give a special friend an unusual present:*
buy a star and name it after them.
Starnames, 0870 1525591

875 **Organize a hen night** and *make sure* you include **stripping Chippendales.**

876 *Get your adrenaline pumping with hand-brake turns and careful skids:*
go rally driving one weekend at Silverstone.
Silverstone Rally School, (01327) 857413

877 Buy an **original** edition of your favourite daily newspaper from your **birth** date.
By Gone News, (01934) 412844

878 See the Queen live.

Buckingham Palace will tell you where you can catch a glimpse.

Buckingham Palace Royal Households and general enquiries, (020) 7930 4832

879 *Give him a* **real** *boy's toy:*

an opportunity to drive military vehicles, or a go on a flight simulator.

Acorne, (01494) 880000

880 Have a pee in the loos of the Felix Bar in the Peninsula hotel in Hong Kong.

They have the most incredible views over Victoria Harbour – and the cocktails are pretty good, too.

Peninsula Hotel, (00 852) 2920 2888

881 *Walk the Dragon's Back to **Shek O beach** on the southeast side of **Hong Kong** island: the view is **fabulous**.*
Guided walks with Dr Martin Williams, (00 852) 2981 3523

882 ***Check out how promptly your man pays his bills.***

Is he a control freak who pays them immediately (preferable) or does he procrastinate until the electricity's cut off and final payments are littering the hall floor? In other words

is he reliable?

883 Meet *someone* through a *dating* agency.
www.pearmatch.com or www.clubsirius.com

884 *Sleep with **every** sign of the **zodiac** and see which **suits** you best.*

885 *Learn to be flexible:*
don't be **thrown** if he changes plans
(with good reason) at the last **minute**,
or if a **friend** feels ill and suddenly
wants you to go to hers for dinner
instead of eating at yours.

886 Don't be *scared* to ask for what you want.

*This applies to every aspect of your life –
from your relationships to your job.*

887 Drive a bus *or a van.*

In other words drive something big, in which
your sense of space and size is challenged.

888 # Start a business.

(Or develop a business idea if the thought of branching out on your own is too daunting.)

889 ### Join a dodgy local club

and see if you meet anyone interesting there.

890 # Chant *positive* affirmations to yourself in the *mirror* every *morning* for a week.

See if your life/outlook improves as a result. Try 'I must, I must, I must improve my bust' or 'I am, I can, I will' or 'I love myself, I love my life'.

891 # *Play the lottery.*

(And be nice to your friends if you win.)

892 ## Be a tour guide.

You know, the person who holds the mike at the front of the coach.

893 Catch the *bouquet* at a wedding.

894 Make *love* on the roof of a building.

Spend Saturday afternoon watching golden oldies:

895 *Pillow Talk*
starring Doris Day and Rock Hudson

896 *The Apartment* **starring Shirley MacLaine and Jack Lemmon**

897 *Some like it Hot* **starring Marilyn Monroe, Tony Curtis and Jack Lemmon**

898 *Ben Hur* **starring Charlton Heston**

899 *Mr Skeffington* **starring Bette Davis**

900 *Rebel without a Cause* **starring Natalie Wood and James Dean**

901 *Cat on a Hot Tin Roof* **starring Elizabeth Taylor and Paul Newman**

902 *Houseboat* **starring Cary Grant and Sophia Loren**

903 *Gilda* **starring Rita Hayworth**

904 *Twelve Angry Men* **starring Henry Fonda**

905 *Rejuvenate yourself*
with some **ayurvedic** treatments at the
Ayurvedic Clinic in New York. The
soothing music, pastel walls and
herbal remedies will **rebalance** your senses.

The Ayurvedic Clinic, (00 1) 212 581 8136

906 *For that certain 'full' feeling,*
try butt plugs during sex.
Available from any good sex shop.

907 Be a well woman.

Get regular smears to test
for cervical cancer.

908 *Develop green fingers.*
Garden.
It's very therapeutic.
If you don't have an outside space, grow
some herbs in a kitchen window box.

909 Buy some *Top Gun*-style mirrored aviator sunglasses.

Read these *feminist* tomes:

910 *Backlash*
   by Susan Faludi

911 *The Female Eunuch*
   by Germaine Greer

912 *The Beauty Myth*
   by Naomi Wolf

913 *Stop worrying for one day.*
See if you can do it.

914 Treat a *couple of friends* to dinner at a restaurant for no *good reason.*

915 Play football in the park
with friends on a summer's evening.

916 **Give an irritating hopeful
the brush off with:**

*'Do mirrors look away
when you
approach them?'*

917 Write him a porny letter.
Post it to him at his place of work.

918 Learn

(preferably not through bitter experience)
that just because a guy wants sex with
you, it does not necessarily mean that
he wants to get to know the real you.

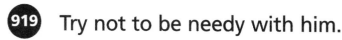

919 Try not to be needy with him.

It's not that attractive. If you're
feeling needy, look to your friends
for empathy and support.

920 *Don't always be
the one to
initiate sex.*

If you do, after a while he won't bother
and you'll start feeling frustrated.

921 Learn to be a **good** listener

*to your friends. It'll stand you in
remarkably good stead for the big
romantic relationship of your life.*

922 *Learn not to tell him*
every tiny detail
of your day.

Edit your streams of consciousness.
In other words, *don't be a bore*.

923 *Make sure he has your best interests at heart.*

Will he **support** you in a project you're interested in that has no **direct impact** on his **life** and happiness?

924 Play a round of golf. Or go fishing.

Participate in a sport you've always found incomprehensibly dull. Then, if he's a fanatic, you might be able to see it from his point of view.

925 *Re-do your CV.*

Make sure it's as excellent and job-winning as possible.

926 Get in a taxi and shout, 'Follow that taxi!'

927 Spend the *day watching* nothing but *soap operas*:
Brookside, Coronation Street, EastEnders, Neighbours and *Emmerdale*.

928 Break off an engagement.

929 Masturbate while travelling at 70 mph.

930 *Do something heroic:*
haul a child that's out of its depth out of the sea; take the rap for something you didn't do; or get a friend out of a tight spot.

931 Jump into a swimming pool fully clothed.

932 Attend the first or last night of the proms at the Royal Albert Hall.

Royal Albert Hall, (020) 7589 8212

933 Deal with an *irrational fear* like the fear of

spiders or flying.

(Apparently, if you eat a spider you'll never fear one again. Rather you than me.)

934 Give the brush-off to someone you despise: say 'How do I dislike thee? Let me count the ways.'

Then stick one finger up. They'll get the message.

935 *Admire a full rainbow ...* *well, half a rainbow, i.e. a 180° arc.*

936 *Go and watch a court case at the Old Bailey.*

937 Tell the **truth** to a **girlfriend** who's going out with a rat.

Tell her why she's too good for him.

938 Learn every *rude gesture* under *the sun:* the Italians have quite a few (wrist in crook of bent arm, bent arm's fist clenched up, middle finger erect … you get the picture).

939 *Invent a* recipe *that people* ask *you for.*

940 Do an all-night sci-fi marathon: *Star Wars*, *Star Trek* or *The Planet of the Apes*.

941 Take a *gondola* up the Grand Canal in Venice at *sunset*. *Gaze* at the magical, *grand palazzi shrouded* in mist.

942 *Give him the thumbs down in style. Say:*

'It's a big world out there. Put some effort into avoiding me.'

943 *Go on a luxury cruise.*

Cunard Cruise Lines, 0800 0523840

944 Be a modern-day Fred Astaire and Ginger Rogers and go to *swing dance lessons.*

Try not to break your leg – you get thrown around a bit. But it's great.

Central London Dance, (020) 7224 6004

945 Know where you stand on swinging.
Just in case he asks later.
(Swinging: also known as wife-swapping.)

946 Go *bowling* with *friends one evening.*

947 Write a personal ad and see if anyone attractive responds.
(Always ask for a photo.)

948 Throw away your mobile phone for a week.
Remember how we all used to live? Isn't it peaceful?

949 Root around **other people's** possessions at a car-boot sale

– and buy some priceless junk.

950 *Get your eyelashes dyed*
blue-black and free yourself from
having to put on mascara every day
for a while. It's great for when
you go on holiday. Waterproof mascara
is such a drag to get off.

951 Take a stall at your
nearest market and
peddle all your old clothes.
Or, if you're particularly good with
your hands, make something to sell.

952 Develop an alias and
create an alternative
history for this **other self.**

953 Spend a summer afternoon watching a friend or boyfriend
playing cricket.
Don't just guzzle the white wine and neck the strawberries. Instead, find out how the game actually works.

954 Go out with someone much posher than you
– or vice versa. See how the other half lives.

955 *Hang wallpaper.*
Then you'll know why people pay so much for interior decorators.

956 Take a boat to the incredibly beautiful Grotta Azzurra off the glamorous island of Capri in southern Italy.

957 *Spend two weeks getting some cheap winter sun on a beach in Goa.*

Thomas Cook Direct, 0870 5666222; or Going Places, (020) 7222 8835

958 Attend a different-race wedding. *(Indian or Jewish nuptials are great.)*

959 Get a Christmas tree

for your home – *especially* if you live alone. *Decorate* it in your favourite colour. (It's good practice for the *kids* later ...)

960 Sort out *your life:*

clean out the attic; file all your papers; chuck out old rubbish. Create some order out of chaos. (Get in a feng shui expert if you really want a Zen living space.)

Feng Shui Consultancy, (020) 8870 0230

961 Write a *limerick* about yourself.

962 Know what a dead body looks like

– TV doesn't count.

963 Spend a *winter* afternoon reading all the latest *glossy* magazines in bed with a cup of hot chocolate *topped* with copious amounts of *whipped* cream.

964 Dress up
as Elvis

and go with a bunch of friends
to an Elvis evening at Jailhouse Rock,
in Hornchurch in Essex.

Jailhouse Rock, (01708) 444408

965 *Change
a nappy.*

966 Turn old skirts
into *cushions*.

967 Take him to a sex shop and buy him
anything he wants.

Put on your make-up to the best tracks from the 1980s:

968 *'White Wedding'*
by Billy Idol

969 *'Kids in America'*
by Kim Wilde

970 *'Don't you Want me Baby?'*
by the Human League

971 *'Jump'* **by Van Halen**

972 *'Girls on Film'* **by Duran Duran**

973 *'Relax'* **by Frankie Goes to Hollywood**

974 *'Who's that Girl?'*
by the Eurythmics

975 *'Like a Virgin'*
by Madonna

976 *'Tainted Love'*
by Soft Cell

977 *'Chain Reaction'*
by Diana Ross

978 Wake up one *morning* and *fly* somewhere *unexpected* by the end of the *day*.

979 See the *world* from another point of view and behave in the opposite way from normal: if you usually *spend, spend, spend,* then resist buying that pair of shoes. Or vice versa: if you tend to be cautious, indulge in an *impulse buy.*

980 *Spice up your exercise routine with something unusual: try*

belly

dancing.

981 *Get ready to give in.*
A marriage works on compromise.

982 # Remember:
it's never too late.
This refers to everything, but particularly
whether you really want to march up that aisle.

(983) *When you've **found** him,*
*don't **think** about what you're*
*going to **gain**, but about what*
*you're going to **give**.*

(984) **When you've found him,**
stop thinking as a single person
but as a couple, instead.

Put 'us' before 'me'.

(985) *When you find him,*
remember to make an effort and still
see your friends. It'll give him space and make
him realize that he's not the only
element in your life. Not only that but your
friends will soon feel hard done by if you give
up your life to your perfect boyfriend.
(In any case, if things go wrong, they'll be
the ones to pick up the pieces.)

(986) # Sack someone.

Even if it's just your *cleaner*. Learn how to
let someone go *nicely*, so that they leave
with some *dignity* without *feeling* too bad.

987 *Listen*
to good old-fashioned entertainment on Radio 4.

Desert Island Discs, The Archers *and the* Today *programme are all excellent.*

Radio 4 is on 92.4–94.6 FM

988 Get yourself photographed at a party by a society magazine or newspaper.

Top marks for *Tatler, OK* or *Hello!*

989 Work out just **how much** you love him:

Does he hog the duvet?
Does he starfish diagonally
across the bed? Or snore?

If he does any of these things and disturbs your sleep patterns, can you put up with it? In other words: would you rather be with him than not?

990 Give yourself a
Veronica Lake-style
glamorous hairdo: dry your
hair in large pink rollers and emerge
looking like a film star.

991 Pour **three drops** of water
on the triple divide pass in
Glacier National Park in Montana.
One drop will end up via the
Mississippi River in the Caribbean Sea,
another in the Pacific and the last in the
Hudson Bay near the Arctic in Eastern Canada.

992 Vow never to *fake* an
orgasm ever again.
If he's not good enough to give you
a good time, why stroke his ego?
And how will he ever learn?

993 **Refuse a lift by saying,**

'Go in that thing?
Wouldn't it be more comfortable

on a pogo stick?'

994 Wander around the
Plaza de Armas
and Cathedral square
in Old Havana, Cuba.

995 When you've found him,
talk, talk, talk
about **anything** you think
might bother you later.

996 Visit a desert island like *Ko Poda* off Krabi in Thailand.

997 **Get a camcorder** and film yourselves having sex. ***Don't** lend the video to a friend by mistake.*

998 *Play the* Lottery *in a foreign country.*

999 Spend one Saturday or Sunday
completely
naked.
*(Obviously it's best not to
go out when doing this one ...)*

1000 *Teach him* **exactly** *how you
like to be masturbated.*

1001 Say, 'I used to be an
exotic dancer.
The money was
GREAT,'
to your future husband.
If he's shocked, do a thousand
more things before marrying him.